I0114079

MARRIAGE DOESN'T WORK

· NEITHER DOES DIVORCE ·

#exposeTHEelephant

Thanks to:

My Boys ~ I Love You, I will

#ALWAYSLoveYOU ~Dada

My mother / My father

Sisters / Brothers

Friends / Colleagues

The Ghostwriters

The Jokewriters

The Comedians

The Musicians

The Artists

The Masons

The Illuminati Party

The Prognosticators

The Pontificators

Lastly...The Ex

Marriage Doesn't Work

Note:

The stories in this book are gruesomely true. Any resemblance to your story; however, is simply just coincidence, just know that you're not alone.

If there is any small inkling of resemblance, I'm sorry you had to go through that.

If you are still out there suffering in silence, my prayer is that you will find your path.

◆▸

CAPPING:

CAPPING in social media refers to:

CAPITALIZINGeveryOTHERword, *Specifically for the use in the digital realm and social media titling and tagging.*

CAPPINGgoesAGAINSTallGRAMMERrulesINtheENGLISHlanguage.

In a digital world, the double space to start a new sentence has disappeared from the rules of Grammar, namely to save storage space, as the extra space is just wasted storage and doesn't really improve readability.

In a social media digital world, spaces take up, well, space, and they aren't very useful in social media especially with regard to building tags and making them readable. There are many cases where individuals create a long tag consisting of several words, ex: **#thisisanexampleofnotcapping**, *and the* **"Case"** *of the lettering makes it impossible to read and comprehend.*

CAPPING solves this problem by making the tag or title readable and easy to comprehend, ex: **#THISisANexampleOFcapping** *-or-* **#THISisOURpresident.**

CAPPING *is beginning to take shape and be used in social media, and was invented by a computer scientist who found the solution while building social media websites and followings, after doing extensive research and inventing a solution to the problem.*

Examples of **CAPPING** *can be found being used in several social media forums.*

Contents

The Perfect Family Has Questions

Stories from the Marriage and Divorce Empire

Solutions

Divorce Court Jeopardy

Multiple Choice

Random Therapy

Marriage Doesn't Work

Intro

What the Fahrvergnügen

"I can't imagine spending the rest of my life with one person; especially someone that I don't like very much."
~Toby Fireboy FickenStar, Random Ghost Author

◇◇◇

WARNING, DISCLAIMER: Swear words, Trauma, Violence, Abuse ... you know the stuff you love to read about...

◇◇◇

I suppose that some type of "rating" system would ban this book from the eyes and minds of the sensitive, but who the fuck cares. Seriously, who has the right to say that some words are harmful while other words are not if they have the same meaning and intentions.

Colorful words just simply get the point across a lot fucking better, and that's my opinion. Additionally, these stories need to be told. This is a topic ripe for revolution just swimming under the surface.

I had true love. In high school. It felt great. I loved that girl. I really did. I still do. I was too young to know what to do with it. Too young to figure it out. Too young to know what I wanted. I was confused. So, I destroyed it. I never, ever had that type of love in my life again. You know the human brain doesn't completely develop until the age of 25.

If you look at the world around you, you will realize that

*" **The human brain doesn't completely develop until age 25** "*

~ Random Fact

not too many people ever get to experience that type of true love. But then again, there are actually two types of love that I know of. There is the young, lustful, love with touching, hugging, kissing and lots of fucking type of love. I don't even consider this to be love, to me this is just lust that lasts a long time.

Then there is the love that everyone has in their heart. God's everlasting love. If you do just a sliver of research, you will find that marriage never existed with early humans.

> *Marriage doesn't make sense for our society today.*

Early humans did not need marriage because it didn't provide any useful value. Now that's smart.

In fact, the earliest beginnings of marriage go back to when Men needed Women to own, as property and ultimately to be slaves. It's built into Spanish law, which crept its way into California Law.

In fact, if you go back far enough in the Bible, Men owned Women. I don't need to tell you that doesn't work for our society today.

Marriage doesn't make sense for our society today, and Neither does its ugly step-sibling Divorce.

So why do people get married. Because guys love power, and all of the power comes from the socket. Women are suckered in by an entire industry that glamorizes the wedding event with shiny, glittery, white satin-ish gluttony filled ceremonies. It feeds into this unreasonable and entitled desire to grab and hoard, more and more, take, take, take, take. And for what? So, the spouse can wear the best clothing, drive the best car, wear the shiniest diamond. Its complete nonsense. Where in the early history of human's do you see this game being played. It simply didn't exist because it wasn't necessary.

Human's invented the Bible. Human's invented Marriage and Divorce. Humans can un-invent Marriage and Divorce. Not so sure Humans can un-invent the Bible, too

Reproduction Venn Diagram

Name: _Yep, that's all there is_____

Date: __Date and Time don't matter_____

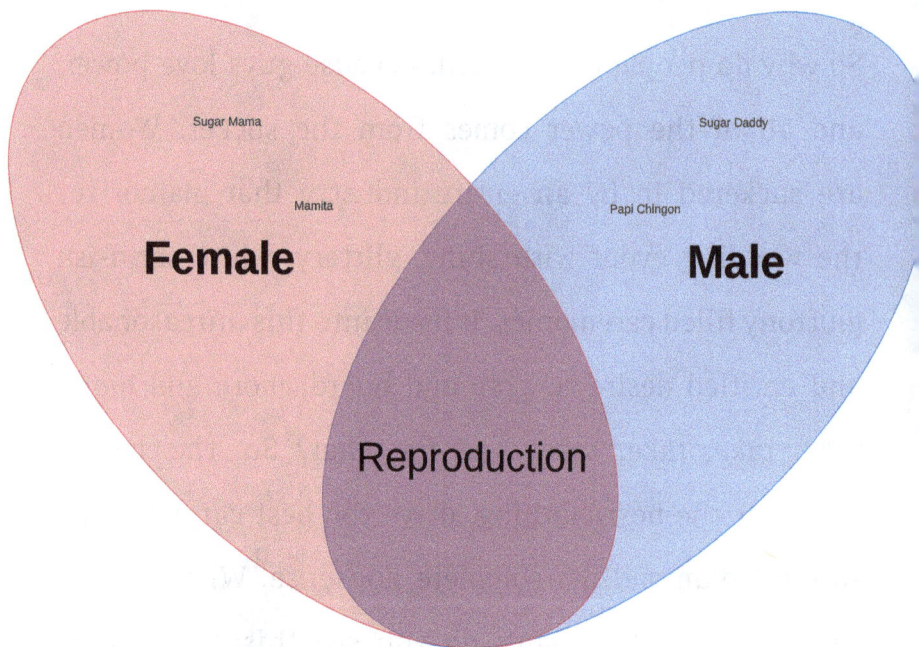

Sugar Mama

Sugar Daddy

Mamita

Papi Chingon

Female

Male

Reproduction

Marriage Doesn't Work

many people have bought into that marketing material.

I'm sorry. I've been told I'm a simpleton. That I don't think deeply enough. I disagree. I do think deeply and fast forward on a lot of my theories. I'm just good at accepting that I have no influence on those fast forwarded, complex pieces. Humans are complex, and they will complicate anything you put in front of them.

If you consider yourself to be a deeply intellectual, highly over educated, theorem prophesizing individual, here is a Venn diagram for you to pontificate over.

Stop making everything so complicated, Men and Women were designed by our Great Creator to come together to reproduce and multiply. Just leave it at that for God's sake.

The problem is Women are using marriage and divorce as a means to an end. It's a game of finding a Man that provides and provides handsomely. They use it to suck money and all that they can from the Man. It plays out time and time again in the courts. Most Women know the law and how to play the game. In California, if a Woman stays married to a guy for 10 years, she gets half of everything of his, for the rest of his life. It's a scam, just like Women using Welfare as a scam. How do I know? Because I would listen to my spouse talk about these things with her friends, although she probably didn't think I was listening. Taking someone elses hard earned income isn't "fair" it's "Financial Rape".

Marriage Doesn't Work

Sadistics

The Twisted Truth

"There are too many people living together in pain, that needs to stop."

~Dr. FuchsViel, Random Ghost Author

Thirty years after my divorce, I fantasize about my no-good, rotten whore of an ex-wife and her despicable, deplorable, detestable parents all contracting a super-severe strain of coronavirus, suffering in unimaginable agony for months and eventually finding themselves side-by-side on ventilators when a power surge causes their lungs to explode. My fantasy is flawed in that such a demise seems too good for them; it's too quick and not painful enough. And I suppose hospitals are equipped to prevent such disasters, but I can still dream.

I can't adequately express the level of my anger three decades ago, when my wounds were fresh. Hell, it was so painful, my wounds are still fresh. There was no doubt in my mind that the bitch and her lowlifes spawned her flying monkeys wouldn't have a chance against me, but I was just sane enough to understand that a judge would likely disagree.

Then, an incredible opportunity to commit the perfect crime and rid the world of my wretched ex presented itself in an instant. I was doing about 40 in my Caddy on Stadium Drive, bordering the Louisiana Superdome, when I spotted the damned slut herself and her wretched but exceedingly bang-able sister-in-law jaywalking across the thoroughfare 20 yards in front of me!

I instinctively accelerated, not wanting to squander

what in my tortured mind was obviously a gift from God. They both looked up and ran for it when either a burst of conscience or, more likely, a lack of balls resulted in my steering around them, saving their worthless lives. They clearly recognized me, but they never thanked me. I'm still trying to forgive myself.

This wretched union we call Marriage, also known as "wedlock," "matrimony," "agony" and "torture" was invented circa 2350 B.C. in Mesopotamia. Mesopotamia, the "cradle of civilization" and the birthplace of misery. Goddamned Mesopotamian bastards! Before inventing marriage, they invented the wheel. They should have quit while they were rolling.

Now for the Juice...

🎭 Scientists have discovered the difference between male and female brains. It turns out women's brains are in their heads.

🎭 According to a new survey, 73% of women would rather watch football than have sex. Fortunately, they don't have to choose, thanks to halftime.

🎭 Facebook is cited in 1/3 of all divorce cases.

Researchers say what starts out as innocent poking often leads to not-so-innocent poking.

😃 According to a new study, the average sex-act lasts 5.4 minutes, which raises an important question. Why do you have to pay for the full hour?!

😃 Demand for sex-robots is surging. Men love sex-robots because they can do anything a real woman can do—and they have a mute button.

😃 According to a new survey, women prefer men with beards. But men prefer women without beards.

😃 New research shows that women who cheat may have a biological reason beyond their control. But in many cases, they are just whores.

😃 According to a new survey, on-line dating is responsible for 17% of marriages. Incidentally, it's also responsible for 40% of divorces.

😃 New research shows that women criticize themselves

an average of eight times a day. Further research shows that they criticize men an average of eight times an hour.

According to a new survey, 33% of women say they feel sad after sex. And 90% of men are unaware of the sadness because they're already in the kitchen making a sandwich.

According to a new survey, 33% of women reported feeling sad after sex. The other 67% didn't know they were supposed to report it.

According to a new study, talking after sex is as important as sex itself for a healthy relationship.

Researchers say men who don't know what to say should at least pretend to listen.

According to a new study, 81% of on-line daters lie on dating websites. Researchers say they were surprised by how many people actually hate long walks on the beach.

I accidentally overdosed on Viagra, but I'm OK. What

doesn't kill me makes me harder.

🎭 According to a new study, women really do prefer men with bigger penises. The complete report appears in the latest issue of the journal "Duh!"

🎭 Scientists say they have determined the length of the average penis. Their findings are based on interviews with my ex-wife.

🎭 According to a new study, women report that they reach orgasm 60% of the time. The other 40% of the time, they rely on men.

🎭 A petition to shut down "PornHub.com" has surpassed one million signatures. Porn advocates say the signers are out of touch with people who are in touch with themselves.

🎭 According to a new survey, Red Lobster is one of the top 10 places that cheaters bring their dates. What better way to let your mistress know you don't give a fuck about her?!

😃 A Nicaraguan manufacturer of adult products is catering to environmentalists with a new line of "green" sex-toys. We already have those. They're called "cucumbers."

😃 A new dating website called "Pinder" helps lonely pets find love. This site is a big hit. In fact, it has already signed up more dogs than eHarmony!

😃 Match.com has created an on-line safety-guide. It offers useful tips, like when you date someone you meet on eHarmony, avoid wearing belts, or scarves, which could be used to strangle you.

😃 According to a new study, watching too much porn can cause short-term memory loss—not to mention short-term memory loss.

😃 There are now several dating sites for celibate people. The most popular one is called "E-What's-the-Point?.com."

😃 In Denmark, a 44-year-old woman who tests sex-toys for a living says she has the perfect job. In fact, she often continues working even after she gets off.

Ref: 1

The Real Truth

"You can't make this shit up, because it's the truth."
~ Duchess von DonnerZunge, Random Ghost Arthur

There is this thing called the "marriage gap", and it stands for the gap in the population of people that are un-married, or not married, for whatever reason. 34% of the United States population has never married, and that trend is going up. Naturally the number of people getting married is trending down.

Marriage is reported, by Wikipedia, to have originated

around 1250-1300 AD (Anno Domini) or CE (Common Era). Apparently marriage was termed after the French word matremoine, which derives from the Latin word mātrimōnium.

This is interestingly somewhat around the same time the Christian Crusades were going on.

Marriage has biblical roots, because in Genesis 2:24, it says that man shall leave his parents, and be joined to his wife, and they shall become one. Christianity holds marriage up as a sacred union of the highest order. Christians, therefore, regard marriage as sacred. However, Martin Luther, declared that marriage is a secular, worldly thing.

What started out as something sacred and beautiful, has unfortunately been distorted by human interpretation of the wife as a slave and property of the man. This goes all the way back to ancient times when men viewed women as inferior to themselves. In Jewish communities a man's wife was selected for him... at age thirteen. The man was considered the head of the household, and his wife was his property.

That's how marriage came to be promulgated around our globe.

Fast forward to present day, and many of the Laws built into our American civil society, still proclaim women to be property of their husband. But, this doesn't work anymore. Women have rights and choices and I can guarantee you that the majority of Women in America, refuse to be "owned" by anyone but themselves.

Marriage doesn't work anymore, especially for our modern society. Most marriages end up in Divorce, and that system doesn't work either.

If we look at the last ten years, we see some subtle trends.

Even more interesting, is the fact that in twenty percent of all marriages and intimate partnerships ~ couples abuse each other. TWENTY PERCENT. This can involve verbal, physical and other types of abuse. Physical abuse in the form of slapping, hitting, shoving and other assaults.

Emotional abuse in the form of verbal threats, insults, humiliating and degrading remarks along with other controlling behaviors. Abuse can be subtle and often starts out small and gradually gets worse with time. The longer the marriage or relationship, the harder it is to get out. Our society has been trained so much, that couples ignore, dismiss and deny aggressive behaviors in their partners. Everyone gets into disagreements especially when in relationships, but it's when the disagreements turn into arguments, and arguments turn into aggressive behavior that our society has trouble detecting. And as we will learn in a forthcoming chapter, our bodies physically and genetically adapt to the trauma in order to withstand it, making us more numb and able to withstand more pain over time.

This is the one area where adults just don't know how to care for themselves. What society has become accustomed to as "Normal" for partners to connect and have relationships ... is just so wrong.

" **On average, more than 1 in 3 women and 1 in 4 men in the US will experience rape, physical violence, verbal & mental abuse, and/ or stalking by an intimate partner** *"*

~ Random Fact

Domestic violence and Domestic abuse can happen to anyone; it does not discriminate. Abuse happens within heterosexual relationships and in same-sex partnerships. It occurs within all age ranges, ethnic backgrounds, and economic levels. And while women are more often victimized, men also experience abuse—especially verbal

DOMESTIC ABUSE DOESN'T STOP DURING LOCKDOWN. #YOUARENOTALONE

and emotional. The bottom line is that abusive behavior is never acceptable, whether from a man, woman, teenager, or an older adult. You deserve to feel valued, respected, and safe.

Domestic abuse often escalates from threats and verbal assault to violence. And while physical injury may pose the most obvious danger, the emotional and psychological consequences of domestic abuse are also severe. Emotionally abusive relationships can destroy your self-worth, lead to anxiety and depression, and make you feel helpless and alone. No one should have to endure this kind of pain—and your first step to breaking free is recognizing that your relationship is abusive so you can get out.

There are some easy ways to spot abuse. These eat away at your self-esteem and how you feel about yourself. Some examples are name calling (stupid, dumb-ass, loser), derogatory nicknames, putting you down, harsh

NATIONAL DOMESTIC ABUSE & VIOLENCE *HOTLINE*

1-800-799-7233

~ An Important Number to Keep in your Contacts. You are going to need it.

www.THEHOTLINE.org

criticism, yelling, screaming, scolding, embarrassment, dismissing your feelings, insults, sarcasm, control, shame, monitoring you and everything you do, spying, decision control, financial control, directing you, ordering you, making decisions for you and angry outbursts.

Emotional abuse and alienation can take on many forms. Some examples are ignoring you, limiting contact, censorship, creating fear and guilt, manipulating feelings, lack of feelings, controlling affection, controlling family contact, controlling your social life, shutting you down and disrespecting you while demanding respect for them.

When you have slowly, quietly been losing your self, you will end up Co-Dependent, where everything you do is to react to the abusers behavior and this way of life consumes you. The abuser needs you and sucks life out of you because it is the only way they can have self-esteem.

Now for the Juice...

🎭 There are over 2000 Women's shelters in the United States.

🎭 There is 1 Men's shelter in the United States[2].

🎭 Over 50% of all marriages in the United States will end in divorce or separation.

🎭 41% of all first-time marriages end in divorce.

🎭 60% of all second marriages end in divorce.

🎭 73% of all third time marriages end in divorce.

◇◇

Apparently we aren't learning our lesson.

◇◇

In 21% of all marriages and intimate partnerships – couples abuse each other.

The average age in Divorce is 30 years old. 60% of divorces happen between the ages of 25 to 39.

Lack of commitment is the most common reason given by divorcing couples - 73%.

60% of cohabiting couples will eventually marry, an over half of those will divorce.

Living together prior to marriage can increase the chance of getting divorced by as much as 40 %

56% of divorcees say they argued too much.

55% of divorcees say there was infidelity.

46% of divorcees say they married too young.

45% had unrealistic expectations.

"*Millions of Men are no longer wanting to get married*"

~ Random Fact

Marriage Doesn't Work

🎭 44% said the relationship lacked equality.

🎭 41% said they weren't prepared.

🎭 25% admitted to having domestic violence or abuse in their relationship.

🎭 Only 6.5 out of 1000 people are getting married.

🎭 Only 9 out of the 50 States recognize "Common Law" marriage.

🎭 "Common Law" marriage claims have a statute of limitations.

🎭 18% of the United States population are traditional Male/Female couples and married.

🎭 7% of the United States population are traditional Male/Female couples and married with Children.

🎭 3% of the United States population are cohabitating Male/Female partners.

Less than 1% of the United States population are cohabitating Male/Female partners with Children.

60% of child births in the United States occur in Unmarried partners.

53% of divorces were initiated by Males in the last ten years.

47% of divorces were initiated by Women in the last ten years.

17.7% of households in the United States are "Single Earner"~ one person working.

10% of households in the United States are "Double Earner" ~ two people working.

1.17% of the United States population, 3,826,670 people, are in a same sex, unmarried household.

1.22% of the United States population, 3,988,041 people, are in a different sex, unmarried household.

🎭 1 in 4 women (24.3%) and 1 in 7 men (13.8%) aged 18 and older in the US have been the victim of severe physical violence by an intimate partner in their lifetime.

🎭 Intimate partner violence alone affects more than 12 million people every year.

🎭 Almost **half** of all women and men in the US have experienced psychological aggression by an intimate partner in their lifetime (48.4% and 48.8%, respectively).

🎭 Most female victims of intimate partner violence were previously victimized by the same offender at rates of 77%

🎭 Nearly 1 in 10 women (9.4%) in the US have been raped by an intimate partner in their lifetime.

🎭 81% of women who experienced rape, stalking, or physical violence from an intimate partner reported significant impacts (short-term or long-term) like injuries or symptoms of post-traumatic stress disorder (PTSD).

🎭 35% of men reported the same significant impacts from experiences of rape, stalking, or physical violence from an intimate partner.

🎭 Two-thirds (66.2%) of female stalking victims were stalked by current or former intimate partners.

🎭 Men who were stalked were primarily stalked by partners (41.4%) or acquaintances (40%).

🎭 The most common stalking tactic experienced by both female (78.8%) and male (75.9%) victims of stalking was repeated unwanted phone calls, voice, or text messages.

🎭 10.7% of women and 2.1% of men have been stalked by an intimate partner during their lifetime.

🎭 Children witnessed violence in nearly 1 in 4 (22%) intimate partner violence cases filed in state courts.

🎭 30% to 60% of intimate partner violence perpetrators also abuse children in the household.

" The average marriage lasts only 8 years "

~ Random Fact

🎭 40% of child abuse victims also report experiencing domestic violence.

🎭 9.4% of high school students reported being hit, slapped, or physically hurt intentionally by their partner in the previous 12 months.

🎭 Approximately 1 in 5 women and 1 in 7 men who experienced rape, physical violence, and/or stalking by an

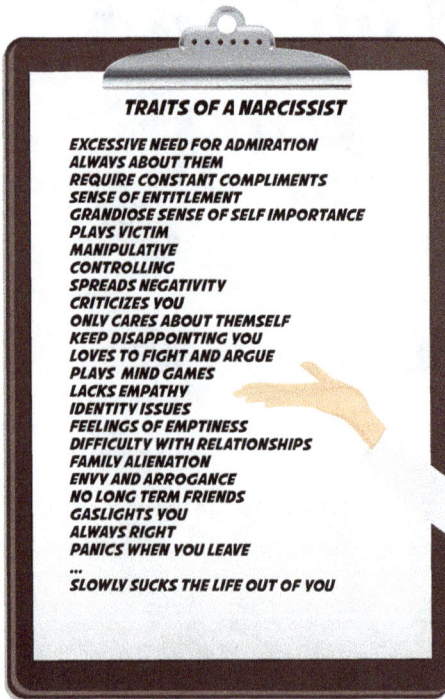

TRAITS OF A NARCISSIST

EXCESSIVE NEED FOR ADMIRATION
ALWAYS ABOUT THEM
REQUIRE CONSTANT COMPLIMENTS
SENSE OF ENTITLEMENT
GRANDIOSE SENSE OF SELF IMPORTANCE
PLAYS VICTIM
MANIPULATIVE
CONTROLLING
SPREADS NEGATIVITY
CRITICIZES YOU
ONLY CARES ABOUT THEMSELF
KEEP DISAPPOINTING YOU
LOVES TO FIGHT AND ARGUE
PLAYS MIND GAMES
LACKS EMPATHY
IDENTITY ISSUES
FEELINGS OF EMPTINESS
DIFFICULTY WITH RELATIONSHIPS
FAMILY ALIENATION
ENVY AND ARROGANCE
NO LONG TERM FRIENDS
GASLIGHTS YOU
ALWAYS RIGHT
PANICS WHEN YOU LEAVE
...
SLOWLY SUCKS THE LIFE OUT OF YOU

intimate partner first experienced some form of partner violence between 11 and 17 years of age.

More than a quarter (28%) of male victims of completed rape were first raped when they were 10 years old or younger.

Approximately 35% of women who were raped as minors were also raped as adults.

With more people working from home, these statistics will go up

The majority (79.6%) of female victims of completed rape experienced their first rape before the age of 25; 42.2% experienced their first completed rape before the age of 18.

1 in 10 high school students will experience physical violence from a dating partner.

Most female (69%) and male (53%) victims of rape, physical violence, and/or stalking by an intimate partner had their first experience with intimate partner violence before the age of 25.

43% of dating college women report experiencing violent and abusive dating behaviors including physical, sexual, digital, verbal, or other controlling abuse.

Nearly 1 in 3 college women (29%) say they've been in an abusive dating relationship .

57% of college students who report experiencing dating violence and abuse said it occurred in college.

58% of college students say they don't know what to do to help someone who is a victim of dating abuse.

38% of college students say they don't know how to get help for themselves if they experience dating abuse as a victim.

Over half of all college students (57%) say it's difficult to identify dating abuse.

36% of dating college students have given a dating partner their computer, email, or social media passwords; these students are more likely to experience digital dating abuse.

Almost 1 in 10 teens in relationships reports having a partner tamper with their social media account, which constitutes the most frequent form of harassment or abuse.

Almost 1 in 10 teens in relationships reports having a partner tamper with their social media account, which constitutes the most frequent form of harassment or abuse.

Approximately 84% of victims are psychologically abused by their partners; half are physically abused and one third experiences sexual coercion.

Current or former intimate partners accounted for nearly 33% of women killed in US workplaces between 2003 and 2008.

44% of full-time employed adults in the US reported experiencing the effect of domestic violence in their workplace; 21% identified themselves as victims of intimate partner violence.

64% of respondents who identified themselves as victims of domestic violence indicated that their ability to work was affected by the violence. 57% of domestic violence victims said they were distracted; almost half (45%) feared being discovered, and 2 in 5 were afraid of an unexpected visit by their intimate partner.

Nearly two thirds of corporate executives (63%) say that domestic violence is a major problem in society; 55% cite its harmful impact on productivity in their companies.

91% of employees say that domestic violence has a

negative impact on their company's bottom line; just 43% of corporate executives agree. 71% of corporate executives do not perceive domestic violence as a major issue at their company.

Domestic violence issues lead to nearly 8 million lost days of paid work each year, the equivalent of over 32,000 full-time jobs.

96% of employed domestic violence victims experience problems at work because of the abuse.

The presence of a gun in domestic violence situations increases the risk of homicide for women by 500%. More than half of women killed by gun violence are killed by family members or intimate partners.

The suicide rate just keeps increasing. Please don't do it. Seek help.

Ref: 3, 4, 5

NATIONAL
SUICIDE
PREVENTION
VIOLENCE
HOTLINE

1-800-273-8255

~ Another Important Number to Keep in your Contacts. You might need it.

www.NIMH.NIH.gov

Marriage Doesn't Work

Why

Marriage Doesn't Work

"Staying in a situation where you are unappreciated isn't called loyalty; it's called breaking your own heart."

~ Wilhelm von SupsenMann , Random Ghost Author

" Marriage Doesn't Work!". I remember the first time I said that, I had my head ripped off by some girl. **"YES IT DOES!"**. We were eating breakfast in a small town called Parker, Arizona. As a small group of friends, we would spend our weekends at the River, having a blast with our water toys, drinking, drugging, hanging out in the sun. That girl was new to the group, and was the last time we would see her. Not sure who brought her along.

I'm not sure why I thought that way, or why I said that. I was quickly put in my place. But I could tell or sense that something was deeply wrong with that girl. She came on the trip with a guy with whom she was very respectful and nice to. Me however; she gave me the look like she wanted to eat my soul. Maybe I reminded her of her ex. idk. If anything the anger that emanated from her scowl was enough to keep me quiet for the rest of breakfast. When we left, the girl I was with commented "what was wrong with that chick". The funniest and ironical part of that story was, that girl was recently divorced.

We are stuck between two worlds, and can't seem to find our way out. The old world where two people fall in love, and get married and spend the rest of their lives together.

Then there is the new world where I think our generation is trying to get to, but with great resistance. I wish we were there now, because it would save so many people from living in pain not to mention time and money.

If we could just teleport to the world where we need to be now, the relationship world would be a better place.

When a boy and a girl meet, or a man and a woman meet, and there is chemistry it's like fireworks continuously going off 24/7. I know, I've been there, in high school. That was an amazing feeling. I destroyed that relationship. I was young, didn't know what I wanted, and was confused. Every relationship I've had with a girl or woman after that has been tumultuous. I don't know why but my picker seems forever broken. Probably because it was never really educated or trained correctly to begin with. Nope, going to church every Sunday won't just magically make it work either.

Children, and I mean humans before the age of 25, should not be allowed to fall in love. Unless of course, we start pounding into infants from birth, Pre-K, Kindergarten and Elementary School, what FEELINGS are. How to understand them, and how to properly interact with another human that also has FEELINGS. Until our babies get a grasp on FEELINGS and how they can be used responsibly, dating at a young age should never ever happen. We all know this is a tall order, because of **PUB-ER-TY**. Kids are gonna do what they are gonna do. Now with technology, it will likely happen at a much faster rate, and with greater stealth.

I knew love. Once. It FELT SOO GOOD. It was pure, raw and perfect. I destroyed it. Because I wasn't mature enough to handle it. I remember by Mother commenting about that relationship long after I had graduated College.

"*Cute!*" she said.

My best friend, when I was in my 30's I should clarify, strangled his wife and shot himself. This was 4 days after my first child was born. Some tell me that my friends spirit will occupy my son's body. If thats true that would be awesome, but I don't really believe that will happen. Ok, maybe I do to some extent.

Some of my friend's friends said that my bestie was having

emotional problems, battling with depression. I know how hard that can be as I struggle with severe depression myself ... every day. But since I manage it successfully, I've never thought of harming myself or others. I also don't think that was the only problem going on.

You see, his wife had been having some type of "friendship" develop at her place of work. But I don't think that was the problem either. You see, I knew them both when they met, and knew and could see how much in love they were. As time passed, they were married and had a child.

When I was around the two of them, I would watch them fight. I think eventually the fighting just got them best of them. After the honeymoon period, people start to change. As people grow older, they also grow and change. They were long past the initial chemistry, feel good honeymoon stage in which they loved being around each other, holding each other and fucking all the time. They had reached a point of divergence.

I never thought my friend would do such a thing as to take

another person's life. I thought he was too intelligent for that. I'm obviously still in denial.

I cried that day, I cried hard. I still tear up when I think about it. I miss my friends. They were my best friends. We went everywhere together.

They left behind the sweetest little girl who didn't deserve to grow up without a Mommy and Daddy. I am still sad and I want them back. I want that baby girl to see her parents again.

I see her on Facebook from a distance and all I can remember at the funeral for the wife, in the back of the crowd, was her fragile little voice crying *"I want my mommy!"*, hands cupping her face, buried into the graceful clutches of one of the mothers best friends.

I wish I could fix it.

But this could have been prevented. If these two wonderful human beings had not been brainwashed into thinking that they had to get married and stay married forever. They each had a soul and a spirit that deserved to grow, love and thrive, whether together or apart. Those beautiful souls are dead now, and there is a hole in my heart. Whenever I hear an old school classic moto guzzi motorcycle rumble, or when I see an old classic restored Porsche, a restored Pinzgauer or an old restored VW pickup truck ... I think of them and pray for them. I know that God has them now.

If you take two people, and they fall in love, it is forever a beautiful thing. Until they fall out of love. Look, people grow and change. It's bound to happen, so enjoy it while you have it. But don't commit yourself to a lifelong hell by not recognizing that people grow and change. Whatever you do, don't get married, because that will just destroy you and your mate.

How does marriage destroy people? If you, and I'm talking about you, not your mate or ex, have any self-worth, self-esteem, peace, serenity, devotion, ambition, career direction, creativity, productivity, sense of humor, zest for living, confidence, integrity, patience, passion, kindness, optimism, communication prowess, loyalty, love for every living thing, kindness, sincerity, generosity, care for the planet, care for all living beings past/present/ future, sense of adventure, tolerance and... spirituality... kiss it goodbye. When you are legally bound to someone, all of the best traits that have or could embody you will slowly be sucked out of you.

Kind of like a massive bag of rice your back, with a hole in it, dropping one piece of rice at a time, slowly, benignly and unbeknownst to you. Until, one day, you wake up and realize, wait a fucking minute, what happened to me? I mean, the real me?

Marriage Doesn't Work

Neither Does Divorce

"Just wait until you discover how your ex-partner is now caring for someone else. In my case, that was actually a good thing."

~ Wanda MehrSchittekatter , Random Ghost Author

Here's the difficult truth, and the elephant in the room. Lawyers and Judges make a shit ton of money off of the divorce empire, sometimes putting people into the streets, bankrupting both parties, until the Judges and Lawyers have all the money you worked ever so hard for, your entire life. They take what you had prior to divorce, and they keep taking for years after your divorce. It's their livelihood, it's a complete waste and it needs to stop.

Judges, Lawyers and the "Divorce Empire" is just a cesspool of elbows and assholes. The sooner you realize that, and accept it, the less pain it will bring. Unless you got lucky like I did, your legal team will do everything except help you. Opposing counsel will do everything to destroy you.

Judges and Lawyers don't care about your kids. They are so buried in their legal processes, pleadings and maneuvering, they don't give a shit. If you aren't on their retainer and they aren't billing hours against you, they won't ever give a shit.

Judges and Lawyers are expensive. Some require a minimum retainer up front, before they even do anything, and there is no way to gauge if they will do the right job for you. It's a total waste. Once they blow through that $5000 retainer in a few weeks, you will get a friendly email saying you need to bring your retainer balance back up to

> **" Find the Judges, Lawyers and everyone else in the Divorce Empire that are going to be "On Your Side" "**

~ Random Advice

$2000 or $3000 for them to keep working on your case. It's complete bullshit, but they charge you anywhere from $250 to $400 an hour. One lawyer I know of, was billing his time out at $1000 an hour.

Judges and Lawyers and all of the other actors in the "Divorce Empire" are all different. Find the ones that will be on your side. Yes, I said "On your side". Judges, Lawyers, Mediators, Arbitrators, Therapists, Counselors, Court Family Investigators (CFI), Parental Responsibility Evaluators (PRE), Child Protection Services (CPS), Department of Human Services (DHS), Police, Firefighters, Teachers, Doctors ... and everyone in between are ... people. People have opinions and beliefs, and those beliefs come into their careers. Those opinions, perceptions and beliefs, even when completely false, will be used against you.

If you are a Male or a Dad, make sure you find a law firm that "likes Dads" and "Men" and will fight on your behalf. Find CFI's and PRE's that are "Dad Friendly" or

"Man Friendly". And believe it or not, you can't choose, but hope you get a Judge that is Dad and Man Friendly. They have opinions, and will use the Law to completely fuck you, if they aren't the slightest bit on your side. It happens every day. I know some divorced Dad's that got a fair deal, and I know some divorced Dad's that got completely, unethically and unbelievably fucked... and that fucking lasts a lifetime.

It is no secret that in the divorce empire, the cards are stacked against Men and Fathers. If you are a Man or Father, you've already lost before you even get to court, so you need to over-correct. You can read about what to do in the stories.

If you are a Female or a Mother, you should do the same.

Judges and Lawyers, despite what they will tell you, make up shit and stir harmful discord between otherwise amicable divorcees. Whatever civil co-parenting relationship you had or planned on having, the Judges and Lawyers will drive a vast and dreadful gargantuan crevice between all parties, and you will find yourself in the middle of a completely made up and bullshit "he-said she-said" string of lies and horror stories. People other than you will be making lifelong, legally binding decisions for you and your ex, ... and your children. You can guarantee the outcome will be bad.

Keep in mind, Judges and Lawyers don't take an oath of honesty in the courtroom, only you do. They can spin, articulate, conjure up all kinds of bullshit. They can ruin your life is so many ways, it is literally inconceivable. And there is no recourse for them. You will see this in the real-life stories later in the book. The shit the legal system gets away with is unconscionable.

I was in an abusive relationship and had to get out, to protect myself, and then my kids. I had a reason. I knew going in that it didn't matter how horrible the divorce was going to get, any day free from the monster was going to be a good day for me and my kids – regardless of what was to come with the divorce.

It's totally fucked up, but until Judges and Lawyers and the entire divorce train is stopped, you are going to need legal counsel. My ex and I filed divorce papers together amicably. That's where the kindness stopped. She wanted everything I owned now and into the future, even though she didn't deserve it. After the first trial, she found another lawyer, and started a stream of legal bullshit to take my kids away from me. And it was never about getting more parenting time, she just wanted more money. You see how fucked up that is. She was willing to destroy the boy's relationship with their Father, just so she could have more money to spend on herself every month.

Another elephant in the room? There is currently no accountability system to ensure that Alimony and Child Support payments are spent on exactly what they were designed for, such as rent/mortgage, utilities, food, gas, transportation. That's right. That ex of yours can do whatever the hell they want with the money, including going on vacations and spoiling their new squeeze. And there ain't nothing you can do about it. This needs to stop.

I was researching lawyers in my area three years before filing, unbeknownst to her. You can read the story later, but it was time. I found a "good" and highly rated legal team through social media. YOU NEED TO DO THIS TOO, until Judges and Lawyers are completely eliminated, you have to do this.

If you have children, especially had them with your ex, you will need to FIGHT LONG AND HARD FOR THEM. Because, as adults, it doesn't matter what happens, you will have to accept your journey. But the kids. The kids WILL be affected, and if you don't start fighting for your parenting rights strong and hard in the beginning and all the way through the divorce, your children will be harmed. There is enough pain in this world, you should work extra hard to make sure your children don't unnecessarily go through more pain because of your divorce.

The main problem with marriage and divorce, is both

parties had no control of the outcome before they got married. There were no boundaries set, no commitments, no concessions, nothing to help them plan 'in the event of divorce' ... which is highly probable as the statistics show. Every relationship should have that difficult decision-making process up front, before the first kiss or first fuck. And that should be it. Because there is no agreement up front, the divorce empire has a heyday will your life and your money... and that shit lasts forever.

Who were you before the marriage and before the divorce? All of those traits that you had before marriage and lost, are going to be reversed during marriage and if not then, during your divorce. You will unknowingly find yourself, and your ex, and the legal system, partaking in the awful side of human nature. You will have no choice but to be dishonest, mean, angry, rude, conniving, strategizing for war, disrespectful, impatient, greedy, pessimistic, cruel, unmerciful, ungraceful, malicious, petty, quarrelsome, selfish, unforgiving ... and unloving.

Your job, after marriage and divorce, is to find yourself again. All of things you were robbed of by marriage and divorce need to be re-discovered before it's too late. You wasted so much valuable time losing everything, you need to enjoy what is left of your life while you can. And life, as you will re-discover, is worth living, especially if you have children and the joy that brings to your life.

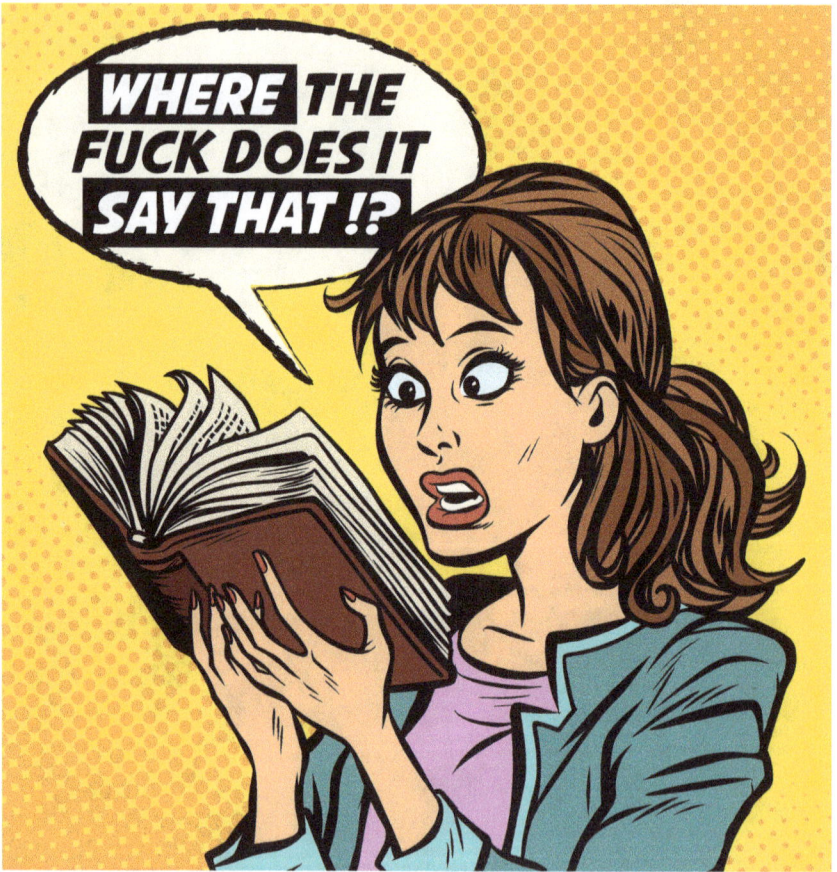

Marriage Doesn't Work

Religion

On Marriage

"You can't be married and be equal. The Bible says so."
~Lord FunkenButter, Random Ghost Author

I'm not a big fan of religion. You will see my perspective when I tell this story. I love my parents. I love my family. But it has taken a long time to get here.

My parents are from the church of the brethren in Kansas. Mennonites. A small sect of religion that emigrated to the United States after the rise of Protestantism in Europe. I was doomed to be a ward of the religion from birth.

You have to remember that back around the time of the Protest against the Catholic Church in Europe, books didn't really exist except for the Bible, and the only people that knew how to read the Bible were the church leaders. Power in the hands of a few. A pretty fucked up power, in my opinion. Thank God we have enlightenment and education of the masses now in the present day.

I think "religion" has misled humankind far away from the intent of God. I believe that the God, the Good, the positive force wants our souls to be happy and co-exist with other good souls. Take away all of the modern day shit we have to deal with, the money, the material things, the material world ... and our souls would just simply seek God, Good, Love and Happiness.

Peace and Harmony would prevail. What else would there be to do. When I started trying to see the God, the Good in every person I meet, life became so much more enjoyable. I started to see how we are all connected.

My parents were married in College and are still married today, over 50 years. My grandparents, on both sides, were also from Kansas and were married their entire lives, over 50 years.

They were all products of the late 1800's and early 1900's. I have a ton of respect for all of them, they endured a lot of bad shit. They survived the depression. For Christ's sake, my grandmother was burying money in coffee cans in her garden up to the day she died. They were taught to Fear God, and the Bible is the word of God. And Jesus was their lord and savior, the son of God.

The Bible says to get married and stay married. The Bible also says that the "Man" has to be the leader, and the Woman must follow the wishes of the Man. Apparently, in order for a marriage to work, according to the Bible, there can be only one leader... the Man.

You can already see how this isn't going to end well.

Here we are now, post-vicennial (After 2020), and I'm

sorry, but the mass of society is now educated and it doesn't take a genius to figure out ... that ain't gonna work. Humans are independent souls and beings, and being in a relationship that you can't leave, where both parties are trying to be the leader, where both are seeking to feed their soul, to be themselves, and seek out connection to the spiritual, is not a relationship that will work and also allow those people to thrive.

I know that we have a spiritual side and a need to connect to the spiritual force in the universe. For God's sake, the ancient civilizations were even doing this. Where we went screwball was when someone decided that the Bible was the only word, the only way to connect with that spiritual force. Prayer works, but not because of religion. Prayer works simply because we are meditating and tapping into the spiritual force in the universe. Not because a religion says it does.

I get it. Religion was used in large part to control the masses, for behavior control, to keep the masses acting toward Good human behavior. I think going to church and hanging out with people that are similar to you is a good exercise at feeding the soul. But as soon as you start citing scripture I immediately think you are a fool and are missing the point completely. Good people hanging out with Good people is a Good thing, a God thing. As soon as the Bible takes over, dictating what humans can, and can't do, telling you what is right and wrong, is when the Bible starts to be a bad thing. The same Bible that says Godly people can't love Gay's or Lesbian's, or Trans or anyone else in the alphabet soup. Where is the Christian love in that? This is the same Bible that creates a Gender dominated society, the same Bible that causes death and war, the same Bible that creates a multi class society, us vs. them.

I didn't go to biblical scholar school, but I'm smart enough to see that the Bible has caused so much pain and hell on earth. I'm smart enough to know that the Bible is not the word of God, but the word of Man thinking he knows what God wants. Humans use their intellect in powerful ways, and no more has this been done on such a monumental scale as the Bible, distorted by Man's so called intellect.

Do you really believe that a priest or pastor has more intellect and knowledge than you, to the point of believing that the Bible is the truth, the way and the life? In your heart, is that true? If you're saying yes, you are still brainwashed. I'm sorry, and perhaps it isn't time for you to see it yet. And that's OK too.

A friend of mine (He/Him/His) has a family member (They/Them/Their) that "hates" Him. They have hated him since the day he was born. They told him they hate him.

He can feel the hate energy when he is near them. It just seethes from them like a big ball of "Don't come near me you pestilent low piece of shit dirty fool" hate energy. He has come to accept it. He has come to learn that hate is their issue and not his. But that has been devastating to him his whole life. They are also Christian Fundamentalists. The bad kind. The kind that professes Christian Love but

"Hates" certain other aspects of the human race, such as people that are "beneath" them. The type of person that would say "I just can't find room in my Christian heart to love you". That is so fucked up. I don't understand how "religion" that follows any "Bible" can be said to be God loving and leading people to seek out God, when it simply perpetuates hate which is the deepest opposite of God, the opposite of Good.

Religion has had a profound influence on Marriage in our society. I'm not convinced it has been the greatest thing for any mind, any body or any soul.

Marriage Doesn't Work

On Divorce

"Divorce is a sin. The Bible says so."
~ Duke Fick Dichan, Random Ghost Author

Religion and Divorce don't mix. Never have, never will.

In fact, in some religious circles, getting divorced is a Sin. This single principle has keep more people in bad Marriages and has probably led to more pain and violence in relationships... than should have ever occurred. The Bible says that whoever marries a divorced Woman commits adultery.

Where is the reciprocity in that? Ok then, it is safe to say that whoever marries a divorced Man commits adultery? Whatever. This is just another example of where the Bible is full of shit.

There have been studies that show that the less religious people are, the more likely they are to divorce. Hooray for them, they are probably the happiest people.

The Christian Emperors Constantine and Theodosius pretty much wrote the modern Bible. I would love to know what the fuck was going through their heads when they did that. I get the behavior control, but come on, some of it is complete bullshit. I mean, Henry VIII of England basically told the Catholic Church to fuck off in the 1500's, just so he could get a divorce/annulment.

Apparently, no-one got the message.

In the 1200's, Catholics said that married persons sin mortally if they don't plan on having offspring. I can see the need stemming from the God given gift of reproduction.

" *If you don't get Married, You can't get Divorced* "

~ *Random Fact*

Reproduction is a good thing and is obviously God Given. But why did Religion think they had a lock on it, and how to control it. We've been severely misled.

I suppose then, it is a sin to fully concede to one's self needs, desires and requirement to live and thrive in the grandest form whatever. This pursuit of "self" would seem like a God Given thing and be a good thing.

In fact, the United States Constitution clearly states We hold these truths to be self-evident, that all **MEN**, which includes all MEN and **WOMEN and everyone in between**, **ARE CREATED EQUAL** by their Creator, with certain unalienable rights, that among these are Life, Liberty (Freedom) and the pursuit of Happiness (Thrive-lihood)".

I know it took a long time to recognize Females are just a part of the "MEN" statement in the Constitution, but we should have arrived at that place by now. Look, it only makes sense, and I don't need to be a scholar to convince you.

Marriage Doesn't Work

You can't be married and be equal. The Bible says so. You can't be equal and be married. The Constitution says so. So why would you even want to do that to begin with?

So then, why does our legal system in the United States then allow and covet the institution of Marriage, and why does it allow the Divorce Empire to reign. I mean, the Constitution clearly prevents it by saying all MEN, WOMEN, and everything in between, are created equal.

Our basic Constitution prohibits Marriage and Divorce. A Marriage relationship is not meant to be equal. A Divorce is quintessentially un-equal, just ask anyone that who has gone through it. Yet, no-one seems to want to talk about that Elephant in the room.

One thing is clear, the Religious institutions that force good human souls into the "Fairytale" Marriage hell-scape, certainly are not taking responsibility for their actions by saying that once you're in, you can't get out ... because it's a sin. What a bunch of assholes, seriously.

> **" *Marriage is the number one cause of Divorce* "**

~ *Random Fact*

I don't know one modern, educated person that would take an honest, objective look at Religion, Marriage and Divorce and not say wait a minute, that's complete bullshit. Who would want to put themselves into that entrapment of hell for so long. That's a fate worse than prison, death or hell for that matter.

Religion created this problem of Marriage, so why can't they just let it go, so we, as humans, can live closer to God's plan, our Creators plan for our lives and the greater good.

God is good. God, our Creator, as I understand him, gave us Love.

There is a force in this universe, and I believe it is a force that pulls and unites everything for the greater good.

Then there is the human will. The dark side that unfortunately seems to show itself in the "bad" things that humans do.

To think that God, good, and love is to be given and used with only one person, is extremely selfish, and I don't believe that God intended us to Love in that way. Just my opinion. Human's are funny and sensitive animals, and we are unfortunately shaped by our surroundings, or societal influences combined with paranoia. Then there is that little God fearing sheep within us that just feels comfortable following someone else's lead.

God gave us animal attraction for a reason. So we could reproduce and multiply. Thats it. For nothing else.

Just like the other animals on this planet. To think that it is to be skewed to serve another purpose, such as Marriage, is just plain delusion. I have yet to see all the other animals on this planet getting stuck with each other for the rest of their lives, with only one wearing a shiny rock taking the lions share of the money and getting all of the attention. You also don't see other animals from the same brood on this planet fighting with each other, unhappy and eventually killing each other physically and spiritually.

Marriage Doesn't Work

The Unfinish Line

Equality, sad but true

"Womens liberation ruined it for those of us that want to be "kept" Women and "stay-at-home" Moms.

~ Wanda MehrSchittekatter, Random Ghost Author

E qual, not special. Remember what the = sign really means, and what it reveals. Too many people display this bumper sticker yet only understand one side of the equation.

We are at a sad place in society when it comes to relationships, and that includes Marriage. We are at a cross-roads and we don't know which way to go. Many of us don't know where to go, so we are just waiting it out to see if a path appears.

"If same gender people want to get married and have a contract on their heads, I say let them" – said from a certain social media networking group that most likely had preconceived notions about gender equality or inequality. Maybe they will have more success than the different gender marriages. However, the trend on same-sex marriages is going down, maybe because they saw the light.

It is sad what Moms do to the Dads anymore. If only they could just be civil and work as adults and co-parent their children together. It's not the child's fault that they couldn't stay together as a family unit. This partner bashing has been brainwashed into most Women's minds to just take everything a Dad has as far as money or anything. I'm glad my exes were civil, and we did great jobs co-parenting our kids.

Shout out to all the bitter, vindictive, immature women

out there. Y'all rock. You know who you are, the ones who listen to your dumb-ass friends instead of communicating with your significant other (S/O), who accuse your s/o of all kinds of bullshit when you know damn well it ain't true, who deprive your child's Father of seeing that child come into this world, who deprive your child's Father of giving that child his name, who threaten to take the child away whenever you don't get your way, who use the child against the Father whenever he doesn't blindly follow along with your petty bullshit, who ignore your child's Father when he tries to check on both the safety of his child and your dumb-ass, who prevent your child's Father from taking an active role in teaching his child, who refuse to let their child's Father be anything more than a cursory presence in his child's life. Here's to you, all you petty, childish, insecure, selfish Bitches. We Fathers, who bend over backwards trying to be good Daddies to our children, sure are ever thankful you Women exist, despite the gap in inequality that you rage forth with.

Its all about equality, as long as it is truly equal. For

example, a feminist once posted "get rid of Father's day, it's offensive to same sex parents, and single Mothers. Stop the patriarchy and ban Father's day!" This is one sided and incorrect. If you want to ban Father's day, then we need to ban Mother's day as well. Because Mother's day is just as offensive to same sex parents and single Fathers. Being equal requires reason, common sense and logic.

Dating sucks these days. You can't look, you can't touch, you can't even comment. If a glance makes someone uncomfortable, you are harassing them. Yet, I see Women's eye's prowling, scanning and quickly glimpsing all day long, everywhere I go. Women are just sneakier at it than Men.

I'm sorry our society isn't as equal as everyone wants, but that isn't my fault, and I think we are at least on a path to get there now.

I call it like I see it. And here are some thoughts that I know are shared by many Men voiced through your favorite social media platforms.

Women want too much in our society. And these aren't my words. I didn't invent this. Ask any guy.

The majority of Women in our society are angry, bitter, immature, unreasonable, un-civil, vindictive, revenge seeking, one-sided feminists, man hating, money hoarding, grab all you can, find a man you can suck off of, use and abuse until you can go prowling again for a bigger, better deal. Oh, and make sure you get a new Land Rover before you bail.

People get married for the wrong reasons these days. I wanted kids, and my ex wanted a bigger better deal. Her standards we low obviously. But it became clear too early in our marriage that she came from a family of wealth and privilege and carried with her a sense of entitlement into everything she did.

It was all about her, all the time. This became obvious in our marriage as she immediately after marriage grew into a mean, angry, virulent, ruthless, unloving, impatient, uncaring, selfish bitch. Not once, since the day we met, did my #XBM (Ex Baby Mama) ever say "I Love You" and never did she say "I'm Sorry". I was required to say these things pretty much daily. Everyone in my family saw it. It didn't take me long to see it either. In fact, the therapists all called her out on it. It took me ten years to finally accept that I made a marital mistake and to finally leave and file for divorce.

She knew it was coming, but she didn't have the balls to do it herself. But when it came time to file, she insisted she be the primary petitioner. I know that doesn't make sense. She never had the balls to file, but when it came time to file, she insisted that the Divorce documents be made to look like she was initiating the divorce. She had been to Law School and learned this little trick to file as Petitioner so that you can file motions and attack the Respondent (Father, Defendant) first, and put the Respondent (Father, Defendant) on the defensive. As the Respondent, you are limited to the amount of defensive arguments you can file in a response. Even if the Petitioner is lying about everything, because your defense is limited, it will appear like the Petitioner is telling the truth. It's so fucked up.

This is the problem. Women these days are selfish, and only want one thing - to get their way, all the way, and it's the only way or the highway.

There are some incredibly illuminating support groups for Dad's online in any of the <insert your favorite social media platform here>. Here you read about all of the injustice being waged against Good Dads and Good Husbands at the hand of angry Women.

Men and Women don't really need each other any longer. Soon we will be able to order, with the click of a button, sex robots. We will be able to order the size, smell, feel, look ... anything and everything that we want in order to bring pleasure to ourselves. It makes one curious as to the fate of the human race in such a state. Who will be making the choice to reproduce? Where will the breeders come from? I've heard some say that the wrong people are reproducing. Well, who are the right people and how do we get them to reproduce to keep the human species going? Where is the equality in that? While we are at it, why don't we just use DNA matching to produce the "perfect" mix of human's we want to represent society? While we are at it, why don't we just remove all of the bad traits of the human, then we will have only robots wearing human sleeves.

Marriage Doesn't Work

It's not a race, or is it

"Comparing your marriage to someone else's will kill it."
~ *Hilde Kondom nach dem Drücken, Random Ghost Author*

I was over listening to a couple of ladies talk with each other at a local coffee shop. I couldn't help but listen it was so interesting.

The minute before that, I was laughing at a photograph of a beautiful woman sitting next to a crocodile. It looks peaceful as if they were close friends. The caption read, "Here is a picture of one of the most dangerous animal in the world resting quietly next to a crocodile."

The ladies started talking to each other about family and siblings. Which ones were smarter and more successful than the other. It is like they needed something to talk about.

They started one up-ing each other. "Are your siblings married?" "Are your parents still married?" One answered, "It would have been 49 years last week." "OMG that's awesome."

Really. We are not being true to ourselves when we engage in this type of discussion.

My parent's got married in college and have been married for over 50 years. That just doesn't happen anymore but when people get married, they somehow start comparing themselves and their marriage to marriages of old. It is as if it is a race to see who can stay married the longest. Ya, marriage is hard, but that doesn't mean it should be a race if it doesn't make sense and doesn't make you happy.

There is so much pressure on couples to get married and stay married. Then once they are in, the pain of separating has been made so unbearable by the court system, that couples that should not be together anymore, can't leave, causing even more pain and frustration.

It's not a race people.

Marriage Doesn't Work

Therapits or They're~the~Pits

"We talk about clients to other therapists all the time."
~ Billy Arschtherapeut, Random Ghost Licensed Therapist

Anytime you see a ton of people popping up in an industry as specialist or freelancers, even whole firms, you know there is a healthy skim game going on. Marriage counselors, Family Therapists ... whatever you want to call them are everywhere.

They are just like Lawyers. There is a ton of money to be made, and that's all they care about. It's all about the skim. How much money they can suck off of you to earn a living.

The legal system, mainly Divorce, is only setup to serve this purpose. If you've been through Divorce, you understand. Everything in a Divorce can and should be handled without Lawyers... but it doesn't happen that way because the opportunity to skim a lot of money is too big.

Therapists are very much needed. They are the shit sweepers that follow the parade cleaning up everyone's shit, including the horseshit and bullshit thats left behind in the wake of fun and destruction.

The same goes for "Marriage Counselors". I should know, I've been going to Marriage counselors since the day I was married. Well, not exactly the day, but within a couple of months of getting married, my new beautiful and beaming bride started dropping the MC bomb. "Would you be interested in going to marriage counseling?" "I think we should go to marriage counseling." It was almost as if she already knew that before getting married, she was going to need some help.

So, we went to Marriage Counseling a lot. We went through a bunch of Marriage Counselors. I even went to my own therapists to help me change my side of the street and keep it clean. My bride never really went. She would show up for a couple of visits and then fire the therapist because he/she wasn't doing what my bride wanted. In fact, out of all of the attempts to get both of us into counseling, I look back and realize I am the only one in the relationship that ever really went to counseling. I am the only one that owned my shit and worked hard to change. She never went. She never owned her shit. She never changed, even after Divorce.

I will say that going to counseling helped me process what the hell was going on, and helped me figure out what I needed to do, in order to remain sane and true to myself.

A good friend of mine once told me that "Marrieds" usually wait until their kid hits kindergarten, then that's when they split. Sure enough, by the time my oldest was in Kindergarten, actually just after that and before first grade, is when I left. My youngest was only 3 years old in Pre-School. I couldn't wait any longer, the pain was unbearable, and I just couldn't take anymore.

"What is your love language?" Who the fuck cares, and who is dictating how and when you should show your love to someone. This is just another book written by therapists to get you to change who you are, to fulfill someone else's wants. It's forcing you to be un-true to yourself. The last therapist I saw, with my spouse, told us, "We don't use Love languages here, because they just don't work". I don't know why I had to pay a therapist to tell me something I already knew to be true in my heart. I guess my bride needed to hear it from a "qualified?" Professional.

Now for the Juice...

There are some things your therapist will never tell you. Some examples of those things?

🎭 They always suggest weekly meetings are better for you, when in reality, they are just trying to maximize their skim intake. You know, weekly recurring revenue (WRR). It's just a living for them.

🎭 A therapist will never tell you the truth or what they are really thinking.

🎭 "That sounds interesting", is therapy speak for they got bored and didn't hear a word you just said. You stopped talking and now there is an awkward pause they have to fill.

🎭 Therapists don't take insurance and they don't have to abide by HIPAA privacy laws because of that fact.

🎭 Therapists do talk about you to other therapists, even though there are laws against it. Some therapists share your stories with their spouses.

🎭 A therapist will never say "I Don't Understand". "I Understand" is what they are paid to say.

🎭 Therapists are not paid to work harder than you. If you just sit there and stare at the wall, they will stare with you, and get paid for it. There is really no incentive for them to figure your shit out.

🎭 Therapists don't fix anything. They just listen.

🎭 Therapists see nothing but broken homes, broken Marriages and destructive Divorces all day long. Yet, they will never tell you that Marriage Doesn't Work, and Neither Does Divorce.

Marriage Doesn't Work

Marriage Doesn't Work

The Kids are Alright

"Children are resilient, they do recover."

~ *Mama gibt keinen Scheiß, Random Ghost Author*

O ne of the last therapists I went to helped me realize the single most important thing about facing Divorce. I was in so much Fear over it. My kids. She told me that "Kids recovery quickly. They are resilient."

I needed to hear that. I needed to understand that deep in my heart of hearts. It was the golden ticket I needed to proceed forward, just knowing that my kids would eventually be ok. It didn't mean she was right, and kids wouldn't experience the Divorce, but it was right for me at the time, and I needed some reassurance to move forward.

Don't be misled, Divorce affects children negatively. But they do recover. And if you can't take care of yourself, there is no way you will be able to take care of your kids. Just know that simple fact.

You living your best life, is actually better and healthier for the children.

Marriage Doesn't Work

The Perfect Family Has Questions

High School Sweethearts ~ His Story

"Marriage is an impossible promise ~ backed by a legal document."
~Judge Junge WankenViel, Random Ghost Author

Alright, that chapter title may be a little misleading. My family is far from perfect. I have been married for six years and, within that span of time, my marriage has seen its fair share of ups and downs. Some might say that six years is nothing. Others might say it's a lot more than many people make it in this day and age. Maybe it'd be helpful to think of it like this: if my marriage were a child, it would be in first grade. Take that for whatever it's worth. I think that it's worth mentioning that many of my peers' marriages have failed in as much, or less, time. It's not a comparison game, but it speaks to the truth that marriage is damn hard and doesn't fit with our society's makeup any longer. As somebody who is happily married, I can attest to that fact directly. And my wife would agree without exception.

We've shared the sweetest of moments and experienced the highest of highs. It's not an overstatement to say that there have been people in our lives who regard us and our marriage as a fairy tale, whatever that means. On the one hand it feels sort of nice to hear. In a world that seems hell-bent on stamping out any and all semblance of tradition, it feels quite good to hear people say that whatever we're doing seems to be working.

But I'd be remiss to not mention the terrible times we've experienced. We've lost far too much sleep over stupid, petty problems. We've gone weeks without speaking about anything of substance. I've cursed at her, both to her face and under my breath. She's done the same to me (by her own admission). She has stormed out of the house, hopped in the car, and squealed away because of how furious she was with me. I've walked out the door and considered how much better her life might be without me. And I would be lying if I didn't admit that there have been times I've wondered if mine might be any better without her.

It sounds horrible to say. As I'm writing this, I'm guiltily recalling all of the fights, the cold shoulders, the grudges, the resentment, and the pure anger I've felt. Maybe counseling would be useful. Despite all of this, I firmly believe that the good times outweigh the bad, both in number and in meaning. The routine fights that come up between the two of us don't deter me from

> **" I made vows that seem optimistic... no... impossible. "**

thinking that either.

The fact is, I made a promise to her, in front of God and everybody. I made that impossible promise, that I would uphold our vows, to the best of my ability, until we were separated by death. That sounds optimistic. Actually, no. Not optimistic. It sounds impossible. It seems idealistic. Its like the hopes of a naive person who is clinging to the traditions of ancient times simply because he doesn't know what the hell else to believe. I understand that now, I really do. Even so, what person am I, if my word is no good? I'm committed to persistently and consistently being the best version of myself that I can be for my wife and children. Does that mean that I'll be successful all the time? I wish! But if the last six years are evidence of the difficulty before me, then the proof will be in the pudding.

The truth is, I'm probably going to fail. Repeatedly. And so will she. Because that's just the nature of the human reality. The human race, as a whole, is plagued with the curse of failure in literally every domain imaginable. It stands to reason that marriage will suffer the same curse. But if we

> **Relationships are blissful, and marriages are a pathway into deep, dark pain.**

suppose that every other endeavor is worth trying for despite the all-too-real likelihood of failure, then why shouldn't the same ring true for marriage?

If it's so difficult, then why?

Why are relationships so blissful, and marriages are a pathway into deep, dark pain? It seems obvious to a lot of people and many have answers of their own. Usually this comes from specific life experiences. Happily married people tend to think of marriage as super Rad. Divorced people obviously think it's a horrible death trap.

> **" *Marriage will suffer the same human curse.* "**

But I think the question is worth taking a deeper look at. The world is filled with tasks that are difficult, yet they are undertaken anyways. There is something about the difficulty of a task that attracts people to it. People need challenge. Challenges are what push us towards growth. We grow at the edge of our comfort zone. That's what parents often do for their children; challenge them to uphold a certain standard so they will grow.

I won't pretend that comparing marriage to education or child-rearing is the same. It's not, and you don't need me to tell you that. But the principle remains. Difficult things aren't inherently bad and they build character. But they do require that the people who dare to take part in them are actually aware of the challenge before them. It is important for individuals wishing to get married to know the truth of what marriages can be, what they shouldn't be, and what they are actually like.

I don't think I'm speaking just for myself when I say that nobody really told me what marriage would be like. Seriously. Nobody told me ahead of time, "You know, there will come a time when you and your wife actually won't like each other." That was a bit of a shock to find out.

Maybe I was a little more aware than others. I remember thinking going into it, "I know this is going to be hard, but if anybody can do it, I can." A favorite band of mine, Rise Against, has a song called Swing Life Away. A line in the song goes, "If love is labor, I'll slave till the end." That was my sentiment as I was preparing to enter into married life. Marriage is difficult, but if there's

> **" *There will come a time when you realize you don't like your partner anymore.* "**

anything I'm willing to fight for, it is this.

Even just a year into marriage taught me how idealistic that song lyric is. At first, it sounded super romantic. I mean let's be real. How many of us out there have been in love and thought, "I would die for you if I had to." I did. I honestly still say that I would now. But the problem is that we all like to imagine that we are the hero. Nobody told me that I had to take the metaphorical bullet every day. Because that's what you actually have to do. The every day work that is involved in making a proper marriage work, is fatiguing. Like, truly exhausting.

My wife is, again by her own admission, kind of high-maintenance. I never minded. I loved doting on my wife back when we were dating. I happily abandoned plans with family and friends for the sake of spending time with her. I made up excuses to spend time with her and I loved doing things to show her my love. It made her happy and I was happy to do it. I thought the idea of loving on my wife every day for the rest of my life sounded fantastic. If that's labor, count me in!

Well, six years later, I can honestly say that as a kid, I was misinformed. I never had to actually do that every day. Now, if I'm being a caring, responsible, loving husband, it means meeting my wife's needs. And I don't just mean sexual needs. If it was that simple, I don't think this chapter would require me writing it. This book wouldn't need to exist. What I mean is this: every human on this planet has a set of needs that need to be fulfilled in order to

> ❝ *Define what it means to be worthwhile.* ❞

feel loved. Some people are happy to simply spend time talking, getting to know their loved ones. Others find their needs being met when their wife makes dinner for them and gives them time to put their feet up. Some know they are loved when their spouse gives them a nice, thoughtful gift. Still, others want to sit physically close and want to cuddle.

> ## "A Couple spending fifty years together, bitter and resentful."

You get the point. If I had known going into it, specifically what my wife's needs are, then I would have had a much more realistic picture of what every single day of labor meant. I don't think I would have chosen any differently. Like I said, I was (and am) absolutely in love with my wife. But I don't think it would have been so shocking to me. We didn't know how to identify those sorts of things, and like I said before, nobody told us that was something we had to learn about.

That is only one specific area out of many that comes to mind when I think about the seemingly infinite number of challenges that come with being married to somebody. But it speaks to the greater point that I'm trying to make here: just because marriage is hard, doesn't mean it isn't worth it.

Justifying the difficulty. So that's where the question leads us. What makes a marriage worthwhile? It depends on how you define

> **" *I don't want that.* "**

what it means to be "worthwhile." You can define it in any number of ways. Some might say that a worthwhile marriage is one that brings you happiness. Others might say it's one that lasts. If we're being honest, there are many ways to define what makes a marriage successful and worthwhile. But if we look at the rate of divorce and even marriages that have lasted, but one or both of the people in them are unhappy, it makes sense to think that some definitions of a worthwhile marriage are better than others.

Let's unpack the two examples I just used. If we define a worthwhile marriage as one that leads to happiness, then the moment one or both partners find themselves feeling unhappy, its toast. If we define it as one that lasts, then it may look successful on the outside, but be dying on the inside. That's a sad thought; a couple spending fifty years of their lives together, but being bitter and resentful for most of it. I don't know about you, but I don't want that.

> " *People who live a meaningful life, look back on it with fondness.* "

Let me preface this part by saying that I'm not saying I have the answer. Some claims are harder to make than others. In this case, it's a pretty huge task. But we can look to the things that aren't the answer in order to point us to a general direction that reveals what the answer may be. Also, it may be the case that for some couples, one of the definitions I just mentioned may be good enough. If so, that's fine. Who am I to tell you or anybody else how to live your lives? What I'm doing here is just thinking a little further about the subject that I think most people do.

If happiness or longevity aren't the best ways to define a worthwhile marriage, then what is? I think the answer lies in something that I've spent a lot of time thinking about: meaning. That sounds vague, I know, but hear me out. At the end of the day, that is the subject matter that everything else hinges on. Without meaning, some argue, life isn't worth living. If there is no meaning to life, then why? You get the point, I'm not trying to depress anybody here.

The best way of living will vary slightly from person to person, but the end goal, as far as I can tell, is to live a life that produces sufficient meaning that it justifies that suffering of life. What do I mean by that? Well, life is full of suffering. Nobody will argue with that. Meaning is the thing that people seek, not a contractual relationship. For some, meaning comes from caring for sick people. For others, it's pursuing the thing they are the most passionate about. Being engaged in the pursuit of something meaningful produces a state of being that leads to less negative emotion. It leads people who've lived a meaningful life, as they have defined it, to look back on their life with fondness. It leads people to the conclusion that despite all of the horrible things that they experienced in their lives, (death, disease, betrayal, the list goes on), that it was worth living.

Okay, fair enough. But what about marriage? Maybe you could say that applies to marriage as well. Could it be that the best way of doing marriage is by aiming at having a marriage that produces the most meaning for you as an individual, for you as a couple, and you as a family, without the piece of paper? And maybe that circle of meaning could expand outward from there. What if a marriage was meaningful enough to justify all of the

> ## *Sacrifice scared the hell out of me, and it chose me.*

explosive fights, the name-calling, the regrets, and all of the other negative stuff that goes along with it, without the piece of paper? That sounds like a pretty damn good deal to me.

> ## *"Moving forward without the same values is tremendously difficult."*

What does a meaningful relationship mean to me?

It means a lot of things, honestly. It means having an agreed upon set of values upon which to build our life. It makes far more sense to me than having separate values and expecting our lives to blend into one somehow or another. The idea of one partner valuing family while the other not valuing family is a bad one. In a way, it doesn't really matter what the values are, assuming they are good, as long as they are the same. Then as a couple, you can work together towards something.

I think a question worth considering is what happens when your values don't line up? I won't pretend to have a blanket answer for every situation. They are all unique and each of them would need a close look to determine what may be done. That being said, I think that there is a general idea of what to do. You have to take a hard look at yourself. Do some thinking. Hopefully both partners can do the same because moving forward without any of the same values is a tremendously difficult task.

Sacrifice scares the hell out of me. But if there's anything that I have found to be true in marriage, it's that sacrifice is not only useful, but necessary. There are sacrifices that must be made. The most basic sacrifice begins with your choice to choose your mate at the expense of every other possible person out there. And it goes on from there, getting more complex and more difficult. But willingness to make the necessary sacrifices, doing so with your head high and your shoulders back, is one of the biggest things that can have an impact on the quality of your relationship. It's an act that reveals love. It reveals commitment. It

> ## Excitement, thrill, ecstasy...that's the simple part.

says that your partner is more important than anything else, even yourself. If that doesn't give your partner a sense of meaning, then I'm not sure what else will. And paradoxically, I've found that despite the difficulty, the pain, that comes with the sacrifice, the more meaning I've found as well.

Sacrifice, however, scary, you have to choose it. The sacrifice is inevitable. It will come your way, whether you want it to or not. Many of the failed marriages that I've seen have involved people that were unwilling to face the necessity and depth of the sacrifice upfront. Let me explain. Let's say the sacrifice required for me is to give up extra time spent in the office, working hard to earn money for the sake of more time with my wife. Giving up your career might sound easy, but it is really hard to do. By me not choosing sacrifice, what I am unwittingly doing is making the sacrifice of my relationship with my wife. I didn't mean to choose it. When confronted, I would probably say I didn't choose it. Maybe it's better to think about it as if the sacrifice chose me. Choose your damn sacrifice or it will choose you.

How to actually keep it going? I think that one of the core principles of my marriage that both my wife and I have agreed upon is committing to never give up on us. It sounds cheesy and corny and whatever. But the reality is there have already been so many times that it could have been easy to throw in the towel and forego the difficulty for the sake of something seemingly easier. I mean if we're honest with ourselves, I think we can all agree that the excitement, thrill, and ecstasy that comes along with dating somebody and falling in love with them is simpler than the rest of it. Mixing up my life with hers? Working out complex disagreements? Seeing my wife as having a viewpoint that may very well be more valid than my own? These things are like communism. They look great on paper, but they're a bugger to actually work out in real life.

Unlike communism, doing these things, despite the great challenge, is worthwhile. The process of mucking our way through these things together and finding answers is a thing that actually can produce a sense of meaning. It can foster a sense of closeness. It can enhance or bring back love.

> **" Great communicators don't necessarily need to be married. "**

But there is a danger. Like an actual, real danger present in the argument I'm making. If you're a reasonable person you might be asking, "So what if we're trying our damnedest and it's still not working? Stay together anyways?" There are just too many couples that are failing at marriage. Too many people are living in pain. I'm not blind to the fact that there is such a thing as an irreconcilable difference between two people. Most couples I'm aware of who've cited this as a reason for their divorce have come dangerously close to hitting that point.

I know that some people actually get to this point. I understand that some marriages devolve into hateful, disgusting, semblances of their former selves. Some people become so absorbed in the vitriol that it may very well get to the point that they may never see eye to eye with their partner again. What can be done about that? If a couple like this were to try and stick it out, they'd better both be as committed to fixing the brokenness, both within themselves and in their marriage. If either of them have anything less than a desire to make themselves or their marriage anything less than everything it could be, then it's bound for failure. But I truly do believe that even the most hurt, broken, messed up people could come to a decision. They could decide to do everything

" *Presume positive intent...* "

in their power to rebuild the pieces of their relationship until it could be functional again. Maybe if functional is a possibility, then healthy might be, too. And if healthy, then maybe even meaningful.

A mental technique that I think can be used by anybody for any relationship, but especially for marriage is this: presume positive intent. But, I struggle with this as do millions of others. Truly. On my best days, I have to stave off the temptation to see my wife's words or actions as working against me. This sounds dramatic. Maybe it is. But sometimes people misspeak. Or misinterpret. I'm guilty of both of these things quite frequently. And I ask for the benefit of the doubt all of the time for this very reason. Why shouldn't I give it to my wife. The woman I fell in love with enough to say, "I choose you and only you, always."

Again this is another thing that is easier said than done, but as I've taken it upon myself to do, it has led to strides forward in my marriage. It has been a thing that has maybe taken what might have otherwise been a week long fight, and reduced it to mere minutes. I'm being serious. It takes me asking for clarification. It requires that I become a better communicator myself. It also means I don't have to be married to be a great communicator.

> **"** *In the middle of a fight, I might get a glimpse of her heart, if she has one.* **"**

"Communicate Better. At least try". It means that when I feel offended by something she's said or done, I don't just assume it's because she's out to get me. "We're on the same team," I often tell myself. And it's true. I didn't marry this woman so that I could have a nemesis. I married her because I could see the potential between us. I could see that together we could do awesome things. We both have dreams, and I believed (still believe) that we can achieve those dreams and so much more by doing it together.

Another thing I've been learning to do is to try not to assume I know everything. As I'm sure you can gather by reading this chapter, I am a thinker. I think about things all of the time. When my wife says something that I think is untrue, I can be dismissive. I can cast out her concern without even thinking. Why? Because I know what's actually going on. Because I see things as they really are. Now that I'm writing this down, I feel like my own arrogance is magnified. But if I'm being for real here. I can unknowingly be like this.

> **" As time goes on, the constant pleasure of being in love wanes. "**

Instead, I try (sometimes I fail. Okay so I still fail a lot.)

> ## " The sensation that drove us together, shrunk to the point of nonexistence. "

to presume that maybe I can learn something from her. I refrain from giving an immediate answer. And most importantly I try to just listen. That's the thing that's most crucial to this and it's nowhere near as simple as it sounds. I can't tell you how many times in my own marriage I've found myself hearing, but not listening. Listening means you can actually paraphrase and repeat back to the other person what they mean and have them respond with, "Yes, that's what I'm trying to say." Anybody who's been married for longer than a day knows how this can happen.

When I take the mindset I described above and apply it, I actually do learn things. Whether it's in a regular conversation, or trying to hear what my wife has to say in an argument, I've actually learned something. I learn more about my wife and who she is. I get to find more about what makes her tick. In what ways she has changed over the years. I get to learn about the woman she is becoming and that's an amazing experience. In the middle of a fight, I might actually get a glimpse of her heart.

I get to understand her and what makes her hurt, what makes her feel loved, etc. And it changes me. Not kidding around here. Not just being a romantic. How could it not? As far as I can tell, that's what happens when I actually invest in another person. I get to offer a piece of myself and receive a piece of her in return.

What happens when the feelings go? Something that is a reality in marriage most often is the fact that as time goes on, feelings change. The near constant pleasure of being "in

> ## *You're not the same person I married.*

love" wanes. In my experience, the strange sensation that drove us toward one another had shrunk to enough to the point of seeming nonexistent. It's a thing that's all too familiar to married couples far and wide. I mean, maybe there are a select few who manage to just maintain that without any real effort, but I've never met another couple who says they haven't experienced the same thing.

I find it weird that despite how common this is, we have no idea what to do with it. I mean really, this is the sort of thing that couples who meet up and talk about their marriages say. So why are we all shocked when we experience it ourselves? Maybe we have a narcissistic belief that we are the one, single exception that exists. Or maybe we just think our own love is so powerful, there is no way it could fade.

Didn't see it coming. I think it actually boils down to something a little bit simpler than that. When it happened to me, I didn't notice it. I had settled down into a routine. Maybe you can relate. I became lost in the day to day of it all. And when you get lost in the rhythm of it, not seeing how you get there, it's impossible to see how to get out of it. I think this is the place where most couples find themselves. And it takes one or both partners to notice it. My wife was the first to notice it and tell me about it. I didn't take it seriously. It led to more dissatisfaction, more arguments, more time wasted.

> **You will both leave slashed by a sword.**

Thankfully, I eventually took it seriously. After taking the time to listen to my wife and hear what she had to say, I made some changes. I tried to be intentional. That meant doing the sorts of things that I had forgotten I used to do. Maybe it was just writing a short note telling her I'm grateful for her. It meant doing the dishes for her once in a while. It meant getting a gift for her every so often, for no reason at all. These are the things that people who are just falling in love do so often. Unfortunately, this doesn't last as you slowly slip into a storm of denial.

Of course the feelings are there in the beginning and fade when we stop behaving the same way we once did. We shouldn't be too surprised, right? Yet we are. Then when things are different than they once were, we get mad about it. They feel cheated. "I don't feel the same way that I used to," or "something has changed between us." And it makes sense that we're frustrated. When dating couples get married and stop doting on each other, it leaves each of them feeling a little bit less loved than it did before. I mean in a way, it's kind of obvious, isn't it? It is yet another Elephant in the room.

There's another side of this I want to look at as well. I've seen couples reach a point in their marriage where they actually look at their spouse and realize that they are different than they were when they got married all those years ago. And they're mad about it. They resent them. They feel betrayed or cheated. "You're not the same person that I married." I've changed since my wife and I got married. I'm not at all the same guy I was when we got

> **" If there is infidelity or abuse, get out. "**

married. I mean, I'm sure the most fundamental parts of me are still me, but there are so many parts of who I am that are different. My wife has said that to me before. Thankfully, in my case those changes have been for the better. Some people find that their spouses have changed for the worse. They have become darker versions of themselves. They have developed seriously bad habits. What can be done about this?

I'm not saying it's possible every time. But I do think that there is a good case to be made for open and honest communication here. I mean jeez, if there is any reason to communicate it's this. It means calmly and earnestly making the case to the other person. You probably aren't going to get the results you're looking for by standing six

> ## " Sometimes we make life harder by not acknowledging how to make it better. "

feet away from them and just blurting out something to the effect of, "You're not who you were before and I don't like you anymore!" That seems like the beginning of far too many fights that lead straight to divorce.

What I have found works when confronting somebody with a hard truth is closing the space between you, sitting down face to face, and coming out with the truth. But not the truth wielded as a sword, hacking and slicing until it's accepted. That's just going to be a painful one-

◇◇

This metaphor was used as inspiration for the book's cover art.

◇◇

on-one using swords. You'll both leave slashed to death (metaphorically).

Instead what you have to do is sit down and explain that you don't want to have the conversation. It's painful for them and if you're doing this in good faith, then it's probably painful for you, too. You explain that this is a necessary conversation because you love them and you want the best for them. You firmly, with minimal necessary force, make your case to them. And when their turn to talk comes, have ears to listen. Try to actually listen to what they're saying. God gave you two eyes, two ears and one mouth – use them in proportion. Maybe you'll have to repeat what they're saying back to them and see if you've got it right. If you do, then you might very well have set yourself on the road to recovering your relationship. But you have to want this, or you will tune out.

This seems like as good a place as any to place a disclaimer to what I'm saying. These things may sound idealistic,

> **"Denial of the elephants in the room has to stop."**

and maybe they are, but I think they're true. I've found them to be so in my own life at least. But a precondition is that it takes two willing people. If you're faced with an unwilling partner, then maybe you're facing an immovable object. Then what can you do? I recommend avoiding the temptation to be the unstoppable force that will inevitably collide with it. That's not to say I think you should just throw in the towel. But, as the old saying goes, you catch more flies with honey than you do with vinegar. Beating somebody over the head until your arm is on the verge of breaking isn't going to particularly help.

Another thing worth mentioning at this point comes in the form of an obvious objection: what if there is infidelity or abuse? Then get the hell out. Unless there is true, verifiable evidence that the offender in the relationship is truly committed to changing their behavior and seeking reconciliation, it will only be more harmful to remain in the relationship. Do I think real change is possible? Yes. I think that people sometimes make mistakes, grave ones. I also think, slimly, that it's possible that they wake up one day, are confronted by the truth of the situation and their heart and spirit actually changes. In those situations, again if there are two willing partners, then by all means work to fix the damn thing. But unless that is actually true, unless you're able to in full honesty and confidence say that they have changed and will maintain this change across time, don't go back.

> **" If you peel back the layers of an onion, it's still an onion. "**

The questions, at last. You might have arrived at this point in reading the chapter and noticed another misleading point. The chapter title says that I had questions. Fear not, I will lay out my questions here. But let me first say I admit that I probably do fall on the optimistic

"*Get rid of marriage, licenses and weddings?*"

side of life. I tend to look for the brighter perspective and look for something called hope. My pessimist friends will undoubtedly notice my tendency and remind me that life, despite how we all might wish, is not actually always sunshine and rainbows. I get that. I don't really think it is. But I do think there is a balance between a realist point of view and maintaining a hopeful optimism. Life is damn hard. Everybody gets that. But sometimes we make it a littler harder than it needs to be by not acknowledging how it might be possible to be better. At long last, here are my questions.

Are two heads not better than one? It seems to me like that is a fundamental thing about marriage. If I know I'm a broken and stupid person and that, despite my striving not to be, I still fail all the time, then it stands to reason that making a partnership with another broken and

Marriage Doesn't Work

stupid person might actually improve both of our chances at being less broken and less stupid. The opposite may occur, I admit, but they say iron sharpens iron.

What about the kids? I know a lot of modern conventional wisdom says that it's better for them to not grow up around fighting parents, and fair enough. But it's also a commonly known fact that kids who grow up living with both biological parents in a low-conflict marriage do better in almost all domains of life. Notice I didn't say Marriage in that last sentence. Broken homes, not broken marriages, cause problems. But, in the face of divorce and the scars that leaves on everybody involved, isn't it preferable to endure some scars in order to provide the best possible environment for the kids? Not throwing shade on people who make different decisions, seriously. You know your own children, family,

> **“We are going to have to start thinking in these terms.”**

and situation best. If you're acting in good faith with the best intentions, then I think everything will work out in the end.

Is the argument that "marriage" and the paper contract is archaic and therefore needs to be done away with really a good argument? I mean it was really just forced into our society by Religion, was it not? You hear this from people that have been burned badly. When you're burned badly, it sucks. I get it. I think we've all been burned at some point or another. Some much worse than others. But just because you're burned by fire, doesn't make the fire bad. It just means it was mishandled, misused or should have been avoided. Maybe the problem isn't in the concept of the union, but with the people participating in it. Wouldn't it be better to find out that the problem is within the individual, not the concept, or in the case of some particularly bitter people, the world? At least if it's you that's broken, maybe you can be fixed.

Marriage doesn't work, but neither does divorce? I do

appreciate the acknowledgment of the problem. There are far too many people in life who pretend like the problems we all know exist aren't there at all. That has to stop. Denial of the Elephants in the room has to stop. But I do wonder what the alternative is? Should we just get rid of marriage? No more doling out licenses to wed? No more weddings? Should people even get together in the form of a romantic relationship?

Obviously, that's not a good answer because people will still form intimate relationships and, since every one of us is subject to our own brokenness, we'll still screw it up. If the piece of paper is the thing we want to get rid of, we still haven't dealt with the problem at hand. Relationships will still fall apart and people will still hurt each other. The only thing that changes is the formality and legality of it. But having come from parents who never married in the first place, the pain from every side is still the same. There's just fewer legal problems to jump through to separate, and hopefully less financial destruction on both sides, however unbalanced. We are going to have to start thinking in these terms.

Taking this argument to its logical conclusion seems to me to suppose that if we just did away with the formal and legal institution of marriage, then nothing would really change. Difficulty by any other name is still difficulty. It doesn't instantly make anything go away, but it does at least the inclination to maintain the family as the basic building block of society without a piece of paper to validate your union. It does remove a bit of incentive from a societal level for couples to remain together, but it also allows for truth to be a part of the relationship, and that is far more important to the health of individuals both adults and children.

I may be naïve, but I am also honest and open. These last six years have been really awesome for me. That's not to say that they haven't been the most difficult damn thing I've ever done (parenting a close second, I'd say). Marriage has proven to be far more a difficult journey than I ever thought possible. But meaning doesn't just strike me as something that is achieved by anything simple or easy. It strikes me as being something attained through chiseling away at the worst parts of yourself (usually the chiseling is done by your partner) and making way for everything you could be to emerge. It's damn painful at times. In the middle of the pain, I often find myself questioning what the hell I'm doing there. But after everything is said and done, I look at the man I have become and compare myself to who I was before all of this happened. I gotta say, at least for now, I miss myself.

Marriage Doesn't Work

High School Sweethearts ~ Her Story

"The last thing the world needs is more broken and damaged people."

~ Fräulein Muschikuchen, Random Ghost Author

When I was a little girl I thought about marriage all of the time. I watched my parents fight so much. My mom slept on the couch after a time and my dad either didn't realize what that meant or didn't take it as seriously as he should have. I had just graduated high school and I was preparing for my freshman year of college when my parents sat my brother, sister, and me down to let us know they were going to be getting a divorce. My whole world turned upside down. Grandma and grandpa had divorced when I was little, but that was my grandparents. My parents were never supposed to get divorced. They had plenty of problems, I was definitely aware of that, but I guess I never thought it would come to that. I was wrong.

My parent's divorce was fairly mundane compared to those of many other people. My dad tried for a short time to convince my mother that the divorce wasn't necessary, but eventually he gave up. She moved out. Their divorce lawyer, who happened to be somebody they both knew and respected, laid out the terms of the divorce, custody agreement for my younger brother, and it was finalized on Christmas Eve. Happy Holidays, right?

During the time of my parents' divorce, my boyfriend, who would later become my husband, let me cry on his shoulders, over-talk things until neither of us knew what else to say, and stuck by me far more than anybody else did during this time. My first year of college with him was a blessing. I was sad, angry, rebellious, mad at my mom, mad at my

> **"My parents divorce was finalized on Christmas Eve."**

dad, worried for my little brother, and concerned that my older sister had stepped in to fill the housewife role after my mother had left. I was trying to deal with all of these emotions and plenty more all the while attending classes, doing homework, trying to make friends, have fun, and figure out my relationship with my boyfriend. It was probably one of the most difficult times in my life. A part of me kind of feels that the time where I was supposed to have the most fun and find myself had been taken away from me. Looking back on it now, it was still that time for me, but a dark cloud certainly loomed over it.

So there's my parents divorce story and the reason why I, as a married woman, am not in favor of divorce. Now, obviously my story wasn't as dramatic or horrible as others' stories might be. You always see divorces in TV shows or movies where both sides are all but held apart from each other by their lawyers while they claw for all of the money, the rights, the children, the dignity, etc. Like I just said, my parents' divorce was far less traumatizing than it could have been. But that doesn't mean there was no trauma. It was just less obvious. My

> **"My sister and I still carry emotional baggage to this day."**

sister and I, being old enough to fully understand what was going on at the time, still carry emotional baggage with us to this day. Fear, insecurity, anger, a longing for days long past. My brother, only nine years old at the time, saw his world change in a bigger way. The days of a family united under one household was gone. He was plunged into a sadness that no nine year old should have to try and break free from. Thankfully, our parents loved all of us and there was enough family support to prevent him from being drawn too deep into it. But there are other nine year olds who aren't so lucky.

I know that the "stay together for the children" idea is kind of relegated to the refuse pile of bad ideas these days, but I can't help but wonder how life might have been different for us if my parents had at least

> **" I am not in favor of Divorce. "**

tried to work it out. I wonder what insecurities I might not have had to learn to cope with if my parents hadn't divorced. If my parents had both truly been committed to their marriage like they once had been, would I have learned some of the emotionally bad habits that are a problem now in marriage. I was shocked after I married my husband that when we argued hotly, I would go lock myself in my bathroom just like my mom had done. If she had been able to have difficult and intimate conversations with my dad, would I have still done that?

I'm not trying to say that divorced couples who don't work it out are ruining their kids or anything. Kids from divorced parents turn out alright. They go on to have lives of their own and lead perfectly normal ones. But it strikes me how many of those kids also divorce. It looks like a vicious cycle to me. It rings true in the same

> *The stay together for the children idea is bullshit.*

way that we know that abused people will often become abusers. It's not an absolute truism, but we know that violence breeds violence. Why should the idea of divorce be any different?

What I hope to do by fighting with all that I have for

my marriage is set a different example than the one that I had. I want to be the sort of wife that refuses to hide in the bathroom. I want my kids to see that yes, marriage is super hard, but it's also super rewarding. I want them to know that it's possible to struggle, but eventually succeed. I didn't have that example and I have to admit that sometimes when I see the struggle all I see is eventual defeat. Thankfully, I know it doesn't have to be that way.

Sometimes a relationship has become so toxic that there's no other option, but I'm advocating for choosing a way that will prevent it from getting to that point. If my parents had been willing and able to do so earlier in their marriage, maybe my mom wouldn't have slept on the couch. Maybe my dad would have seen that as the latest sign that his marriage was in big trouble. Maybe there are children out there whose parents didn't have to divorce.

How can this be done? As if there is a single answer.

I wish there was. I wish there was a way to just quickly solve problems as complex as this one. But I do think there are steps that can be taken. Unfortunately, it isn't a simple thing. People like easy, linear, solutions to things. But the truth is much more nuanced than that and we all know that people don't really like nuance.

What I can say for sure is that it seems like when time goes on, people generally rely on their feelings to decide what to do with their marriage. To me this seems like a big mistake. If I were to decide what to do about my marriage based purely on feelings then it probably wouldn't have lasted the first year. It turns out that feelings change over time. Emotions are a fickle thing. They can change on almost unexpectedly and against your own wishes.

> *Some part of me wasn't satisfied with the happiness I felt.*

My husband and I started dating in high school. I know, I know. We're those cheesy high school sweethearts that make people gag when we tell you how we met. But our dating relationship was almost more difficult than our marriage. Well, maybe not, but it was no picnic either! When I think back and remember how much my own insecurities had influenced the early parts of my relationship with him, I am still floored. We fell head over heels in love. But not two months into that, I felt myself withdrawing from him. Growing distant. Why? He was a great guy, especially when I compared him to the other guys I saw around school.

> **Our feelings leave out a key component of who we are... our brains.**

Apparently, some part of me wasn't satisfied with the

happiness I felt. Some part of me felt the need to keep looking. I couldn't explain it at the time, but I suspect that some part of me was afraid of growing closer to him. Maybe I was scared of letting him see my broken parts. I might have been afraid of letting him see how I wasn't everything that he thought I was. So I let my feelings guide me. They pointed me away from him and towards another guy. I ditched him at a football game we had attended together and chased a boy who didn't even want me.

> **" *Guys, your girls are struggling just as much as you are to understand their feelings.* "**

Looking back now, it's easy to see how wrong I had been to let my fear control me. I didn't know any better at the time, but I do now. I have a feeling there are lots of people who still let their emotions guide them all of the time. It's easy to do. It doesn't require much difficult thinking. It means you just act according to what they would have you do. Feeling angry? Lash out against somebody. Feeling sad? Lock yourself away into your room and give up. Feeling lonely? Go find somebody to take away your loneliness.

It's a really big problem because it leaves out a key component of who we as humans are. Our brains. When we choose to simply follow our feelings wherever they go, never stopping to think along the way, we behave more like animals than people. If people always behaved that way, I'd imagine we'd been in seriously rough shape as a species.

As a woman, this is something that I believe I am particularly susceptible to. Not all women are the same, but we tend to feel things more than men. Some men, for sure, are more articulate of their feelings and feel them more deeply than other men, but we as women I think tend to be more sensitive to emotion. This is especially true for negative emotion. It takes a great deal of effort for me to shake the feelings that I get, good or bad, and integrate them into myself. After that, I might have an idea what to do with them, but I grapple with them. I cry over them. I lose sleep over them. I don't often find my husband consumed with emotion in the same ways that I am. And trust me when I say my husband is an emotional man. Like, he is usually the first to shed tears when we come to dramatic arguments.

But even he admits that he doesn't really understand the way I feel when I try to explain how my emotions bubble to the surface. I try the best way I can to express what exactly I'm feeling and the depth that I feel them, but it is seriously hard for him to grasp what I mean.

I'm explaining this because I think that other women might find they relate to this and maybe men who read this might have a moment of insight here. Guys, your girls are struggling just as much as you are, maybe even more so, to understand their feelings. This isn't an excuse, just an explanation. Maybe if we understood our differences more, we'd be a little bit more gracious when we're dealing with one another.

Atill, this is a concern for everybody. There is no one person out there who is fully capable of setting aside their emotions and making completely rational choices. But I don't think we're meant to either. I think our hearts are supposed to inform us in much the same way our minds are meant to. Our brains take in stimuli from the environment and a cascade of effects take place within our minds and bodies as a result of what we see, feel, taste, heart, and smell. In similar fashion, our hearts are responding to emotional stimuli. Often times those stimuli are far less obvious than we'd like them to be.

We react, in an unaware sort of way, to the emotional stimuli our hearts have received. My husband speaks to me in a certain way. Maybe I interpret it, on some level, as being hostile towards me. It's possible it's not even a conscious thought. Yet I react without fully knowing. Those emotions rise up in me and I react with hostility. He hears it in my voice, again on some level or another not fully aware of the heart-level emotions being changed, and responds to me with further hostility. It becomes a dangerous cycle of misunderstanding until eventually we blow up and a full fight ensues. All because we don't fully understand one another on a day to day level.

> " *You can look at your formation as a person as a result of your past experiences.* "

Now take that same concept and apply to it the worst days. Maybe we've been fighting for some time now. We feel frustrated, angry, bitter, resentful. We are caught in the cycle and, in a way, we don't necessarily want out. Then a thought occurs. "Maybe I should leave him." I don't often like to think those thoughts, but thoughts do come unbidden from time to time. There might be a moment upon thinking it, in which I feel like it's a good idea. I have a feeling that I will be happier. And it makes sense. When you're in the middle of some of the worst times in your life, it's logical to presume that if you didn't have to deal with the problem at hand, then you would be happier.

So what happens if I just follow that feeling? What if I let the thought linger and chew on it for a while? Maybe I'll like the idea more and more. Maybe all that's left is the need for one more fight to occur and hit the breaking point. Then, all the time invested goes out the window. All the pain and agony, would be for nothing. All of the sleepless nights, the stupid fighting, the pointless arguments over what to eat and why he can't just choose something or why I can't just say what I want doesn't matter anymore.

My view is that following those feelings without seriously thinking about the idea makes little sense. In much the same way that it might lead people to make horrible career choices, making choices regarding your marriage based purely on your feelings will leave you alone and with little to show for it. God knows the last thing the world needs is more broken and damaged people. That is what you get when you let feelings just lead you around aimlessly.

When Does It Matter?

I mentioned above that casting the marriage aside would render all of the most difficult times you as a couple have endured null and void. That sounds kind of harsh and if I'm just thinking in a practical sort of way, it's not exactly true. Of course, you can always lean on your past experiences, good or bad, and they will have left a

> *Our societies collective mind says the struggle is worth it.*

mark on you. You can use that to help determine your next move in similar situations. You can look at your formation as a person, partially a result of your past experiences, and be grateful for everything you have endured that helped make you into who you are now. I'm fine with that way of looking at things.

But I can't help but to think that if my husband and I were to separate, then I would look back and see all of the difficulty we'd experienced together, sometimes because of life circumstances, sometimes because of one another, and feel like it was all for nothing. Hear me out here. We've stuck it out through some seriously hard times. And I know that six short years is nothing compared to twenty, thirty, or forty years of painful memories that some couples share. Still, if we called it off, I would be stricken at the idea that every time we'd figured out how to overcome our struggles, it would have meant nothing in the end. Because why would it matter? What good would come from fighting through thick and thin, sticking it out together side by side for better or for worse, if during one of the worst times, we gave it up? What good will it have done? Shown to us that we can overcome difficult times? Then why not this one, too?

No. I think that it is better to become better. To learn how to fight together, rather than against one another and to prove to yourself and to each other that all of the fighting

> **"When we used to hold hands in public, I Never wanted to let go."**

is justified when the battle is won. When you can look back as two gray-haired people and look fondly at the life behind you and say with confidence that despite all of the heartache endured and all of the tears shed, it was worth it.

Our society's collective mind is filled to the brim with the idea that the struggle is worth it. There are so many shows and films that embody this idea. The hero, struggling against all odds to defeat the bad guy and save the innocent. Why is that idealized in the form of a film, but not in everyday life? Is it somehow less brave for a man and woman to fight like hell to defeat the odds and save the innocent children from the consequences of a marriage turned bad? Why should that be the case? Why should we find that to be less compelling than Jason

Bourne putting an end to the bad people at the CIA that want him dead?

Disney gets a lot of criticism from the post-modern types for portraying their princesses as needing to be saved by their princes. And I get it. Some of it is completely fair. Some of these portrayals might leave a young girl with the impression that she needs a man to save her. I don't think it's exactly true. But I do think that girls, and women, would be thrilled to know that there is a man out there who would be willing to fight with that same sort of tenacity in order to keep her as his wife. I'm not the type of woman who wants to see women's rights be reversed and for women to be locked away in the kitchen or any nonsense like that. I'm the primary breadwinner for my house, my husband taking on the primary responsibilities of bringing up

> **“ Now when we hold hands, it's just inconvenient. ”**

> ## " *How could I be in this committed relationship, legally binding, with someone that I don't even like?* "

our children while pursuing his career on the side. I mention this only to prove that I'm not forcing some misogynistic worldview that I've been forced into. Rather, I'm a successful woman who is working her rear end off to provide for my family, but also to keep my family whole. My husband does the same, just in a different way.

What's the point I'm trying to make? It's this: there is something inherently noble, attractive, and necessary about a man and a woman who are willing to face adversity head on, whether it takes the form of a dragon, a tyrannical leader, or a darkness that would like to see your partnership dissolved into nothing. And I think that nobility is worth striving for, sans the piece of paper.

Keeping the Spark Alive. This is a tired argument in a way. It has sort of become a platitude. You see somebody who seems to be struggling in their marriage? Just tell them they have to keep the spark alive. Or the romance. Either one works. I remember being told that we had to keep the spark alive during our difficult times by several well-meaning people. But I honestly didn't understand what it meant. When asked, some people would say, "You have to go on dates every Friday night." I was told by a woman I asked that it meant you have to hold hands when shopping, just like you did when you were dating. "You gotta spice things up in the bedroom," one incredibly awkward family member told me. But what if we just don't like each other any longer.

I still don't know if there is a single good answer to this, but I think the idea behind it is still true in a way. If I pull at the idea and let it unravel, I think

> **" Being in love isn't supposed to be this hard, yet it is. "**

> ## " You can't live with somebody for the better part of a lifetime, and always like them, it's just not human nature. "

I get a better idea of what it actually means. My guess is something like this: in order to keep your marriage alive, truly alive like it was when you were dating and everything was exciting and you felt in love, then you have to continually choose to do that. And for some reason it's incredibly hard to do. And why did marriage fuck everything up the way it did. Why can't we just go back to being in love. There is something that happens when you've been married for a time that is frustrating to me beyond all reason. You just get used to it. I miss the days when sitting down at the movie theater with my husband, before we married, gave me butterflies in my stomach and joy that lasted for days. When we'd hold hands in public, I never wanted to let go. Now, when he holds my hand while we're shopping it's kind of inconvenient. I need that hand to grab things off the shelf, you see. I think to myself, "Sweetie, I know you don't need your hands to complain about being in the store, but I do need mine."

Isn't it kind of ridiculous? That your perception of a thing could change so drastically, especially in regards to somebody that you love? It's crazy to me. Why wouldn't it be easier? I can truly understand the mindset of people who find it getting difficult and say, "I don't think being in love is supposed to be this hard." Yet it is. And I've yet to meet another emotionally healthy couple that thinks it's easy. In fact, those that do feel that way, I kind of suspect they will find out how difficult it really is sooner

> ## *I just want to feel loved. I also know my husband can't just snap his fingers and make that appear magically.*

or later.

So why isn't it easy? I wonder if I'm supposed to be with my husband, then why is it so hard sometimes? Sometimes I don't like him. What a thing to say! How could I be in this committed relationship, legally binding, with somebody that I don't always like? Yet here I find myself. And for some reason, I desperately don't want to change it. It seems ludicrous. Still, I think it makes sense in a way. Beyond the obvious answer of "You can't live with somebody for the better part of a lifetime and always like them," it's just not in human nature to do so. I honestly think that if I lived with myself for more than a month I'd strangle me.

We get on each other's nerves, we do things that the other person just doesn't understand. Sometimes these things just take time to grow into, but sometimes they are really significant differences. My husband always argues with me. Seriously, he can never just agree with what I have to say, even if it's something innocent like when I think the weekend has been way too quick. He'll say something like, "Really? It's actually been a long weekend. You had Monday off this week and we've had a lot of quality time with the kids." Nothing makes me crazier faster than when he does this crap.

It's not that he is trying to argue with me, I've discovered that he simply thinks he's holding a normal conversation with me by sharing his thoughts on what I've said. Maybe I look into it too much. But then his friend comes over and says all kinds of wild things and my husband just laughs, smiles, tips back his beer, and agrees. He agrees with him! What the hell?

Living with someone, especially in the context of a deeply intimate relationship even if not married, isn't going to be easy. It's going to take a lot of work to make the thing work. And I think that's the idea behind "keeping the spark alive." It's about putting in the work, married or not. It's about going out of your way when it's much easier to just keep doing what you've been doing. And I don't think it has to be big things either. Some of the times that I've felt the most loved, the most special, is when my husband randomly buys me a cheap bouquet of flowers from Wal-mart. It sounds stupid, but in those moments I know that he is thinking about me. That he really does love me. And in the end, that's all I really want.

Tell Me What You Want. I want to be loved. To feel loved. To know that my husband loves me. But it's more than just knowing that he loves me. I mean, I

> ❝ *We both had assumptions and didn't share them.* ❞

know that he loves me. That's why he married me in the first place. I want to feel it, though. I just want to feel loved. I want to know in my heart, rising out of my chest, that he loves me. That is, after all, what it felt like when we were dating. But I don't want to be doted on just for the sake of it. It's more than doing it purely out of obligation. I don't want him to schedule "flowers" into his iPhone every second Wednesday and do it because that's what he's supposed to do. I want to know that those flowers came from him wanting to give me a gift, no matter how small, to let me know that his heart is set on mine. I think this is what women most often want at the bottom of it all.

I thought about what my husband wants, what men want out of a partner. Looking beyond the crass jokes about sex, I think that men want from their wives what they want out of their friends. They want to be liked. They want a buddy. They also want to be respected for who they are. I've been up front and honest before, in the heat of anger, that I love my husband, but I don't particularly like him right now. I can see him deflate a little bit when I say that to him. I've heard that from friends and read about it in blog posts. Men often feel secure in the fact that their wife loves them. But it's not always the case that their wife likes them.

I talked to my husband about this, asking him if it strikes him as true. He had to think about it a little bit, but after doing so he concluded that he would like to know that no matter what happened between them, that I still thought he was someone worth liking. He wants to know that even when he messes up and says hurtful things, I will still like him because of who I know he is. He wants to be affirmed for the man that he is, despite his flaws, just like I want to be loved for the woman that I am, despite my flaws.

> **A part of growing together is learning each other.**

These are two sides of the same coin, as far as I can tell. Two deep-seated needs that each individual in the marriage have, both of which need to be filled by the other person. It is my job to affirm to my husband that yes, in fact, I do still like him and respect who he is on a fundamental level. It is my husband's job to reassure me and reveal to me the depth of his love. It is this understanding that we have for one another that helps us to know how to meet the emotional needs that each of us have, though we didn't know it for some time. When we made the discovery, it felt like finding buried treasure or a map to Atlantis. Had this been there all this time? What had once seemed like an impossibility, now feels to me like a practical everyday tool that I can use to help ensure my marriage stays healthy.

But we didn't need to be married to discover and use this tool!

On the topic of keeping our marriage healthy, it's been amazingly helpful to go beyond what we both assumed would be true about marriage and instead find out what is true about our marriage. Every person, as well as every couple, has their own unique sets of strengths and weaknesses. When we enter into marriage, we each come with the skills we've developed over our lifetime of becoming individuals. A lifetime. Admittedly, for some, that's not very long. Regardless of your age when you unite, you come bearing all of the things that make up who you are, for good or bad. The truly difficult part is figuring out how to blend your two lives together, all of those things considered.

When we both came into our relationship, having dated for quite a bit of time beforehand, we felt like we had a good idea of what our marriage would look like. Unfortunately, we were wrong. Settling into the same household together and dividing up duties between us was surprisingly difficult. We both still came with at least a few assumptions about how it would work, neither of us having ever shared those assumptions with the other. It shouldn't be a shock to hear that we struggled with that. Figuring out what worked best for us became a much easier task once we figured out what our strengths and weaknesses are.

I'm good at numbers in a way that my husband isn't. It's nobody's fault and he is no less a man for it. It's just how we're made. This means that when payday comes,

> ## Choose love when it's easy. Choose love when it's difficult.

I spend a little more time on the budget than he does. He is a good thinker. He can analyze complex, abstract problems in a way that I can't. I'm no less intelligent than he is, but it does mean that I come to him when faced with big problems that need to be decided on. And there are small things, too. I don't mind doing the laundry. He hates it. He doesn't mind doing the dishes. I hate it. So we have figured out what works for us and what doesn't. He loves to cook. I love to bake. It doesn't mean we don't help one another out, but it does mean that we know how to distribute the duties that come along with being in a functioning household together.

On the other side of the coin, we find our weaknesses.

I'm not good at cooling down after an argument and letting things go. So I need my husband to come to my side, remaining calm and good-natured, and lead me out of my bitterness. He's not good at seeing my perspective when we're in a fight. I have to remind him that I don't need him to fix my problems, I need him to hear where I'm coming from. It's truly difficult work, but it's also some of the most rewarding work that I feel we've done in our marriage. It's led us to a place where we have more tools ready at hand to muddle through the difficulty of marriage and do it together. But getting to the point that we need these tools was extremely exhausting.

Of course these things aren't always as obvious as I wish they were. I wish that I could always have eyes to see when my husband's weaknesses are impacting him. I wish that he could do the same for me. It would sure make things way easier. But part of growing together as a couple is learning each other. It's learning to see the other person in the full picture of what they are, the good and the bad. Through seeing that I can see that maybe there are ways that I can help him become the best version of himself. And he can do the same for me.

And that's the most beautiful picture that I can imagine between a man and a woman, striving together in partnerriage. Two people, who love each other despite all of their differences and the pain they inevitably cause one another. People who, knowing full well that they are entering into a union overflowing with both love and brokenness, decide to weather the storm. You can safely assume that those people will be battered, blown away by the wind, soaked from head to toe in heavy rains, and may even get struck by lightning a time or two. But people who face that forthrightly with their shoulders back and a willingness to stand in the eye of the storm and face the thunder with courage are heroes in my mind.

To wrap up, let me say this: choose love. Don't wait for a feeling to show up or for it to remain forever. The fact is it will not remain or may not just re-emerge. A thing that we somehow intuitively know in the beginning of a relationship and forget over time is that we must choose love. It rings true with our children when they screw up and crash our car into a light pole. We can choose to react with resentment and bitterness or we can choose love. It holds true with our mothers when they lash out at us for changing traditions or our fathers for forsaking the lifestyle they wanted us to live. We must choose to love them.

My mindset, at the bottom of it all, can best be summed up by saying that in order to succeed in any relationship, you must choose love. Choose love when it's easy and when it's difficult. Choose love when you have to decide between sleeping on the couch or next to your partner. Choose love when you have to decide between giving a cold shoulder to your man or sharing your heart. Choose love when it means listening with no agenda to your lady while she sheds tears that make no sense to you. And choose love when you are faced with the most difficult decisions that you have to make about being in a relationship, regardless of marriage.

Now for the tricky part. Did we really need to get married to have this relationship? To create this Family? If I look back at all that we have been through, and all that we have fought for, that piece of paper really wasn't necessary. In fact, if things do get sour sometime in the future, that piece of paper will just make it harder to grow and move on as healthy humans should. While I am all for building a Family and building and nurturing a strong relationship, the fact is that Marriage is a myth perpetrated by Religion. Men don't own their wives these days. Roles have changed. We live in a two -earner society. A Marriage contract just doesn't make sense. A healthy relationship with a healthy Family does make sense.

Marriage Doesn't Work

Stories from the Marriage and Divorce Empire

Prince Charming

"When I met and married my man, I felt as if I had reached the finish line, and was just happy that someone wanted me."

~Sister Greta von Needham, Random Ghost Author

O h hello, I'm a lady human who will tell you a little bit about my marriage. My husband, wait, I'm going to call him my partner. I don't want to have a "husband" I want to have a partner. The word "husband" is very scary and possessive. And, I'm not a "wife" I'm a lady human a lady-man? Which I already established in the first sentence. I also want to establish that I believe being married is absolutely, certifiably deranged. If you take away the good stuff in marriage (Honestly, I've experienced loads of good stuff) but if you take it away the positive (friendship, support, sex) it's a legally binding contract that basically forces you to envelop your partner's problems - from their financial and family problems to their emotional and psychological problems - they are yours now. Congratulations on doubling your problems! Ha, maybe that should be on a wedding card. It says "Congratulations ..." on the front and when you open it up it says .... "On Having Twice As Many Problems! Good Luck!" That would be a dick card, you know a dick move but one that calls out the elephant in the room.

Another insane thing about marriage is, after a while, you expect the other person to basically become a different person. In return, they do the same thing to you. It's so fucked up.

Anyway, before I tell you my story, I'd like to start by saying my partner and I are still together, working on it, trying

Marriage Doesn't Work

to not to destroy one another. We go through extreme cycles which I hope end soon. These extreme cycles feel like a roller coaster your dumb friend made you go on. Your friend is like, "Come on, I swear it's so fun, you're gonna love it." Trust me. Look at all the other people doing it. So, you go on this ride and your favorite part of it, is when it's over, and you barf on your friend and don't feel too bad about it.

> **" I guess we both liked sharing the role of CuntMaster. "**

Our marriage cycles are like this - we get along great - it feels natural and easy and fun. Then... a resentment starts to stir in one of us and, if it's not communicated in an honest way, the passive aggressive punishment begins and whoever is on the receiving end of it is like, "What the fuck is your problem?" Then there's a HUGE argument, where honesty finally rears its head, then the aftermath sometimes lingers for weeks. Then, we go to therapy and work it out and start the cycle again.

Looking forward to this for the rest of our lives!!

We have gone through many phases and have taken turns on being the asshole. I guess we both liked to share the role of Cunt Master. In the beginning it was my husband who was the dick. He just could not admit that I had pissed him off, or if he was jealous or upset about it. It's like he was allergic to negative feelings. He'd have

> **"The person I was before I got married was gone. Disappeared. POOF!"**

this weird reaction and it showed up in insidious and passive aggressive and manipulative ways. He's British, so being upfront and honest is alien to him. But thankfully he's a very willing, emotionally intelligent and open guy and we've been in couples counseling now for a couple of years. Our communication is much, much better. But NOW, if I'm being honest with you, I'm the asshole. He's the cool one. Now I'm the one who is upset over small stuff and get sort of a sick enjoyment out of making him miserable because I have a big, overarching resentment ... and it's the ol' "I gave up everything for you" elephant in the room of every home created by marriage. And, the weird thing is, "WHY did I give up everything for him?"

I call it the Prince Charming syndrome.

I met him in London, as I mentioned before he's British. We exchanged numbers. We started texting. He flew to the states to be with me for a few weeks. It was fun. I had met my Prince Charming. We both put on a great show. You know, the show we all put on when we are seducing someone. It's that "courting" period. It's the "I'm fun and easy going" show, the "ain't no better buttercup out there but mine honey", the "you gonna love my shit", the "my shit ain't like no-one else". After all, all the power comes from the socket, right? We all do it. We both enjoyed each other and it showed. That was some of the best sex I ever had. It wasn't just a sexual connection, it was a very deep intellectual connection and it was intoxicating.

Next, I flew to England to spend a few weeks with him. It was cold and wet, but we still managed to fall in love.... and within six months we were married. BAM. It happened really fast. I gave up my life as a writer in LA and moved to England to be with him. Can you believe that shit? Why was I so willing? I'll get to that later....first, let's talk about the identity crisis I experienced immediately after dropping my life for his.

Within the first week of being married I was startled awoke – realizing that there was this person I was before I got married and... that person was now gone. Disappeared. Poof. I don't think it would have been so dramatic if I didn't drop my entire life to get married AND move to another country. Being an expat alone, is very, very difficult. Most people see it as exciting or exotic (it eventually is) but the first couple of years are brutal. You're suddenly in a new culture where everything is different, from the food you eat to the way you say goodbye on phone calls. English people end calls like this, "Ok, darling. Bye bye... bye bye bye." Or "cheers mate". They say an average of five byes. And cheers is for when you are going to drink to something. It's fucking weird. My point is, I felt like an alien. I can't blame my entire identity crisis on marriage, but don't you worry I'll blame a lot of stuff on it!

> **I even picked the tree I was going to hang myself from.**

First bad choice, moving from LA to England DURING THE WINTER. Living in Los Angeles was like living through a very weird and exciting twelve-year summer, where I only had to wear a jacket once. My skin was always slightly tan, and my hair was naturally highlighted. At some point I'll probably discover I have stage four skin cancer, but I love California. I love the sun, the people, the police chases, I even love how it might break off into the ocean one day I really hope I'm there when it happens. I wouldn't mind at all.

But there I was in England, and after only being there for a week I wanted to kill myself - I even picked the tree I was going to hang myself from. The weather felt like a personal attack on my nervous system. It was grey, rainy, windy and freezing and I was surrounded by people too polite and reserved to complain about it. As I layered my clothes before walking into the freezing cold, I'd think, FUCK YOU ENGLAND, and this negative start to a life in the UK was the beginning of a long transition process.

> **" I even stopped wiping my ass. "**

The last time I remember being happy before it got really bad was on our wedding day. We had an adorable little ceremony just south of London. We had a fiddle player, our wedding attire was really fucking stylish, the sun was shining and my mom only said two things that got on my nerves. But shortly after I said "I do" I became possessed by a very insidious and lazy demon. My drive to achieve was gone. My spark. You know that "thing" you need, not positivity, but what's is it called - oh yeah - the will to live. It vanished. I stopped writing, stopped being

> **_Childrens fairy tales are responsible for all of these fucked up marriages and relationships!_**

myself, stopped talking to my friends, stopped being outspoken, stopped going to twelve step meetings and I even stopped wiping my ass after I took a shit. I'd just pull up my underwear and waddle around for the rest of the day. Books are real fucking boring sometimes and then you end up checking your phone and the next thing you know five years go by. It's fucked up.

Did my husband make me stop doing things I loved to do? No. Did my own actions lead me to this place? Absolutely. And look, I'm aware that it's normal for newlyweds to hibernate and forget the rest of the world, but this was something different. This wasn't just being in love and wanting to spend every second together, it was more than this, it was something that I felt like I was obligated to do. Isn't that crazy?

> *Happily ever after was more like happily never after.*

Getting married and moving to England was the end of my old life and a start of a new one, which sounds normal and to be expected, but I wasn't there. My body was, but my spirit stayed in LA for some reason. Of course, moving to another country was messing with my vibe, it's such a bizarre experience. I assumed it would be easy because everyone in the UK speaks English, but I'd listen to a British person talk and have no idea what the fuck they were saying.

I just found myself spending so much time alone. He worked all day and I just sat there alone wondering, "What in the actual fuck?" And I couldn't legally work until I got the proper visa, so I just sat alone crying. Happily Ever After? More like Happily Never After! Fuck you fairy-tales!

Children's fairy-tales are responsible for all of these fucked up marriages and relationships.

What was even more frustrating was my darlings lack of understanding of what I was going through. He was nice and tried to fix things and make me happy by scheduling fun things to do. He was really sweet to me, but on the flip side he was like "I don't know what's wrong." And it would infuriate me because he changed nothing about his life. We lived in the town he grew up in. The house he'd been in for 20 years. He'd run into friends at the shops. He'd come home and tell me about his exciting day, and I hated him for having a life. Basically, I tapped into some rage I had no idea I even had.

Again, yes, I chose this, but I think when you get married you don't REALLY know what you're choosing for yourself. YOU are delusional and walking into the biggest legally binding contract of your life, and you are completely blind. You have no idea what horror lies ahead, and the scariest bit is - you've committed to it - FOR THE REST OF YOUR FUCKING LIFE!

> *You are delusional as you walk into the biggest legally binding contract of your life.*

The nuttiest thing is, I did this without thinking twice

about it, I just did it. I thought I was the one who had to do ALL the sacrificing. Not sure why, I was financially secure, close with my family and friends, was at the top of my game career-wise and when it came to deciding how we could make it work it was like I was conditioned to be the one to take care of him and put his life before mine.

I mean, he had a great job, a house, and a fun-loving family. And, I didn't think I'd have to live in England forever. The deal was to live in the UK for a few years, save money,

> ❝ *I tapped into some girl rage I didn't even know I had.* ❞

then move to the states. It didn't seem like a such a big deal, it felt adventurous and he was worth it. Plus, I had never met anyone like him. He works hard, he's funny, he's kind, he texts back right away, he's not a gross eater, he's everything I could ever ask for. He's one of those "good ones" you hear about. I'd be nuts to let him go. He was the

Prince Charming all us girls are sitting around waiting for. Ladies watch Disney movies! If Prince Charming shows up, you better fuck his brains out. I'm pretty sure that's what Cinderella did.

Who is this Prince Charming that we dream of anyway? When I think of the Prince Charming syndrome, I think about how I was conditioned, socialized and trained to believe in that fairytale. Which is weird because I have always been somewhat of a feminist. Before I met him, I was convinced that I wasn't going to get married and I was ok with it. I had seriously surrendered to never getting married and was not upset about it. But, I guess the messaging in society is so strong that it even got to me, the self proclaimed "fiercely independent"

> **" *I'm a fiercely independent woman, yet the messaging still got to me.* "**

Marriage Doesn't Work

woman. Maybe it was at night I was dreaming about Prince Charming... that fairytale.

Somewhere awaits my knight in shining armor, on a horse, coming with his band of thieves -or- tribe, to come and literally sweep me off my feet and rescue me from this lonesome life. He is the most handsome man in the world, super rich, good hearted always doing the right thing. Treats all living things nicely. He's a poet, over educated and can make me wet just by listening to him converse – the ones that sapiosexuals are attracted to. I am to be crowned the Queen, and live a life of leisure and luxury, with servants to scrub my feet when I'm tired of walking from the upstairs to the downstairs. You know the one. These stories abound in our culture, often inoculated by marketing, media and movies. Who wouldn't want a Prince Charming to come along and rescue us? Unfortunately, this just isn't real. Even people that are still of Noble descent in Europe can't do this, except for maybe one or two Royal Families. The odds are 1 in 7 Billion that you will find that Prince. Time to wake up.

I think what I'm trying to say is, women are told from a very young age that, "There aren't many good guys in the world, so if you find one who shows interest, it's your job, as a female to sacrifice your life for him. Otherwise, you're a fucking nut-bag. You'd be absolutely crazy to not give everything up for one of the good ones, because there's only like... one good one out there! Oh, and if it goes wrong there must be something wrong with you, you titty toting woman."

That accent. Ooohhhh that British accent that could seduce or sell anything to anyone. I'll admit that is still a large part of the allure. Point being, I felt obligated to move across the world for him. Not only was I madly in love with him, but I was also programmed to be the one to basically end my life as I knew it for him. My subconscious was riddled with messages from society's training pants, and I was willing to do whatever I thought it would take to make it work... because as a woman, that's my job, right? If I wasn't so brainwashed, I could have easily worked out a long-distance situation with him, making it clear that

Marriage Doesn't Work

my career is very important to me and I needed to spend at least half my time in LA. If he needs to be in England for his career, that's great, then he'd understand that I need to be in LA for mine. But nope. The second he implied I should move there to be with him I was like, "Ok, you're a good guy so I better do it my English Prince!" Basically, I volunteered, I chose, I was a cheerleader behind the idea of giving everything up and moving to England so we could be together.

> **" *The odds of finding prince charming are 0 in 7 billion.* "**

The absolute worst of it, besides feeling guilty for not being happy, was finding myself very dependent on him. He became my only resource, both personally and financially. I had no friends, no resources, I didn't even have a favorite coffee shop to hang out at. I spent twenty years in the states networking and working my ass off to make a living as a writer and here I was at 40 years old in a new country with the daunting task of starting from scratch. Guess I overestimated how I could "write from anywhere" - wrong. Sure, I could technically write, but I think when you're a writer with contacts in LA and New York - you need to be in people's faces. If you are out of site and out of mind then, unless you're Shonda Rhimes or Steven King, you're pretty much dead. I was dead!

> **"I don't like being a kept Woman, earning money and supporting myself are very important to me."**

Being dependent on my partner, left me feeling helpless. Even though he was the one that wanted to live in England and has all of the resources for survival at his fingertips. Then he should be the one to take care of us. I didn't even know how to "take the tube" or say "aluminium" properly. PRIV-acy/PRY-vacy, Ga-RAHJ/

GARE-udge, MO-bul/mo-BILE, jagwar/JAG-U-war, AD-ver-tize-ment/advert-IS-ment, SKED-ual/SHED-ual. There are over a hundred objects that are a part of daily life that the British have different names for, such as bathroom/loo, football/soccer, TV/telly, cell phone/mo-BILE, vacation/holiday, gas/petrol, fries/chips, cigarette/fag, sweater/jumper, trunk/boot, tennis shoes/trainers, dude/mate.

If he had moved to LA, I'd be the one working while he freaked the fuck out about how to start from scratch. Point being, I don't like being a kept woman. Earning money and supporting myself has always been very important to me, but after a while there was something about being married that made it "ok' to be taken care of, despite the fact that it made me uncomfortable. I took responsibility for paying my bills back in the states using my dwindling savings account, but he was the sole breadwinner in England.

Maybe a few of you reading this are thinking, "What are

you whining about, you dumb cow? I'd LOVE to be taken care of financially, so I didn't have to work." Well, then go and find yourself a financially stable partner and try it! I think this factors into many people decision to get married, and it stems from the fairytale. Get married, be taken care of, don't work, stay home and lose your fucking mind!

This situation reminds me of a few stay-at- home moms in Beverly Hills I know. Their husbands are wealthy, they no longer work, and they are miserable and a bit nuts. One time at a party, I remember talking to a very wealthy guy at a party and he told me that he "saved his wife from a teaching career." I knew his wife; she was sad and angry. I thought the very thing that would make her feel better is the thing she gave up, a teaching career.

Was this who I was becoming? An ungrateful lady of leisure? Why, in my right mind, a normally very independent, outspoken, and somewhat weird and wild character choose to stop doing the things she loved and just sit at home waiting for her husband to get home from work? Am I some sort of sadist? Deep down, do I want to disappear and be "taken care of?"

Prior to getting married, I had spent the past twenty years working odd jobs before I was able to make a living as a writer. I had two to three jobs at a time, scrambling around to make ends meet and I didn't know it at the time, but I had pride. I lived on my own in New York and Los Angeles, fully financially supporting myself while battling some demons - like alcoholism and even worse - dating guys who didn't own a bed frame. I quit drinking. Yay me. My choice in men slowly got better. Way to go. I got a few big writing breaks. YES! I was on my way, I had momentum, I finally hit a groove and was happy and this is when he showed up. And, without thinking too much about it, I very willingly gave it all up because I thought if anyone was going to sacrifice anything, it was going to have to be me because I'm "the girl." I was a semi-brainwashed woman who had been programmed for years to "find myself a good man" and I found one! Guess that means my life is over! I reached the finish line! I know assuming I was brainwashed by society is a very dramatic thing to say, but I'm gonna say it anyway.

Women choose to sacrifice and disappear and give, and if we don't do those things, we feel guilty. Why? Because we have been taught to. When I was a kid, I had way more responsibility at home than my older brother did. I had to look after my younger sister while he practiced break dance moves in the basement. Do you think he's a professional dancer now? NOPE! And he doesn't even know how to hold a baby properly! He holds them upside by one leg because he never had to learn how to do it! Parents - give your sons just as much responsibility as you do your daughters. Make your boy do some shit around the house

> *" Men have been doing whatever the fuck they want, without thinking too much about it. "*

Marriage Doesn't Work

for fuck's sake!

Roxanne Gay says.... "most girls are taught—that we should be slender and small. We should not take up space. We should be seen and not heard, and if we are seen, we should be pleasing to men, acceptable to society. Look at what the makeup industry has done to us. We can't go outside without "looking" good. Why do guys get to roll out of bed throw on sweats, wear the same t-shirt as yesterday and think it's just ok. I mean all the other dudes in Home Depot are doing it. And most women know this, that we are supposed to disappear, but it's something that needs to be said, loudly, over and over again, so that we can resist surrendering to what is expected of us." This just doesn't fit our society any longer. It's a myth and it is destroying people from the inside out.

This is very hard for men to understand, because they have been very busy doing whatever the fuck they want without thinking too much about it. It's weird, because I fancy myself a "bad ass" and I like to "say it like it is," but if I'm being honest, I have a habit of making myself really small physically and mentally. I weigh 110 pounds and think it's too much. I like being really tiny, taking up too much space is not acceptable. I do not deserve it. I especially feel this way around big personalities who are easily threatened by other people's razzamatazz. When I take up space, I can sense certain types of personalities want me to tone it down, there is no room for both of us. Here's an example: I used to do stand-up comedy back in NYC and made the horrible mistake of dating a very jealous, competitive comic. He used to get visibly upset when good things happened in my career, so I of course sabotaged myself to lift him up.

> **" I sabotaged myself to lift him up. "**

WHY WOULD ANYONE DO THAT?

Michelle Obama says, "Women, we endure those cuts in so many ways that we don't even notice we're cut. We are living with small, tiny cuts, and we are bleeding every single day. And we're still getting up." Yes, we are still getting up. Thank fuck! We are cut, bruised, battered and unbelievably exhausted physically and emotionally, and we are still getting up and trudging forward. I'm happy to announce that I have decided to join the ranks of women who are getting back up. I'm taking my life back. I can no longer be a victim of my own decisions and resent my partner for just being himself, for living his life.

> ❝ *We decided we must be an unconventional couple or else we won't make it!* ❞

And, in return, he can't expect me to forget about who I was before our marriage happened, and happily leave everything behind. Something must change.

We've been together for five years and we've decided that we must be an unconventional couple or else we won't make it. We love each other to bits and I don't want to be with anyone else. I can't imagine not being with him, but I also can't imagine a life where he is the ONLY thing in my life. I need my family and my career and my culture. So does he.

He doesn't want to move to the states, and I don't want to stay in England. He wants to go back to school and focus on work and I want to focus on my career and tap into the resources I have back home. If I continue to stay here for him, I will continue to resent the shit out of him, and it will destroy us. If he resents my decision to finally do what I want to do (live in the states and work) it will destroy us. So, now it's come to the point where HE has to sacrifice by being ok with me going back home. And I have to stop resenting him for not wanting to go to the

> *We gotta be who we are and wish the other person well.*

states. ACCEPTANCE OF REALITY IS NECESSARY FOR BOTH PARTIES. We must give long distance a chance and let the other person be who they want to be and do what they want to do. Why force them into doing something that makes them sad? Why hate each other for not being exactly who you want them to be? It's insanity. Long distance isn't ideal, but neither is living with each other seething with resentment and getting in arguments over dirty dishes and watch to watch on TV.

WE GOTTA BE WHO WE ARE AND WISH THE OTHER PERSON WELL.

Besides, there are loads of unconventional marriages. Especially overseas. I know of a couple who only spends four days a month together. She lives in Hong Kong and She lives in London. And that's not a typo. It works! It's sexy! They appreciate the shit out of each other when they do see each other. Why suffocate a person when you can just miss them instead?

I know this book is about how marriage just doesn't work.

I agree but I also disagree. For the lucky few, it does work. Some couples are magic together. The old couples who have been married for fifty years and still hold hands when they walk down the street, or suddenly start jamming and dancing to a favorite tune from yesteryear. The couples who are each other's biggest fans like Ruth Bader Ginsburg and her husband Martin D. Ginsburg. And those lucky bastards who just got lucky and truly found "the one." Am I one of the lucky ones?

Sometimes it feels that way. Sometimes I feel like I'm the luckiest girl in the world and am so grateful for my funny and kind partner. Other times, I'm googling divorce lawyers. I'm pretty sure he feels the same way.

For us, marriage isn't going to work in the traditional sense where we live together in the same place for the rest of our lives. We are going to have to tweak the norm in order for us to stay together. And it took A LOT of work for us to get to this point. We've been in couples counseling for almost two years. Our communication and lack of reacting to each other has matured into something almost beautiful. Sure, we still have huge fights but we recover quickly.

Before counseling it was impossible to talk about anything uncomfortable. Thank God we've both been willing. And we've both worked on ourselves outside of the marriage. We've taken separate vacations; we have different social circles. We have had to learn to give each other space for the other person to be who they are OUTSIDE of this relationship. When you try to control or fundamentally change who a person is, they don't change, and it just makes you crazy. Let them go, while you're still together and let them be who they are meant to be.

In closing, there is no such thing as a Prince Charming fairytale....that's why it's called fairytale. And there is no such thing as Happily Ever After.... It's just a lazy way to end a story.

The Trauma Informed

"PTSD... Thats what men remind me of."
~Lady Snapdragon, Random Ghost Author

◇◇

TRIGGER WARNING: Domestic Violence, Sexual Assault, Rape

◇◇

Before I met Travis I felt sorry for, and if I am completely honest even felt superior to, the women Margaret Atwood was talking about when she said "Men are afraid that women will laugh

> **The chances of killing me went up 750%.**

at them. Women are afraid that men will kill them."

Until I joined that terrifying sisterhood.

I barely made it out of my marriage alive. When Travis put his hands around my throat and strangled me unconscious the chances that he would kill me the next time went up by 750%. The research proves that stunning 750%-more-likely-to-die statistic. Research also explains why, like me, about 12 million women go back to their abuser each year after an attack involving strangulation. Spoiler alert: It's not because she's stupid.

Travis and I met at church. I could not understand why this tall, beautiful man with jet black hair and crystal blue eyes had any interest in a mousy woman like me. But he pursued and I quickly fell for him. Surprise picnics, long walks on the beach, sex like I'd only read about in books and gifts of jewelry. Three months into it the gift was a ring Travis presented while down on one knee.

> ## "I suffered in silence on my horrormoon!"

Travis said my love brought him to his knees and he wanted to love and worship me there for all of our lives.

Six months later we were married in our church by our pastor and absolutely everyone was thrilled to see this fairytale play out in front of them in real life.

We left on our honeymoon cruise and the first night in our cabin Travis told me "You're mine." I smiled and giggled thinking he meant to have and to hold, to cherish and to love on an affectionate level. What he meant was since he put a ring on it, he owned every part of me and he'd do as he pleased.

And that he did.

The first three nights and days of our honeymoon cruise he kept me tied to the bed, the "Do not disturb" sign hanging on the door. Whenever he came back from the pool or a fine meal or the bar he beat me, he raped me, he starved me and made me tell him over and over "I'm yours."

You would think there was alcohol and drugs involved, but there wasn't, we both lived clean and healthy lifestyles. Sex robots and dolls hadn't been invented yet, and least not full body ones. But that's what I felt like. A lifeless piece of flesh just laying there for Travis to have his fun with.

Day four he went to the ship gift shop. He came back, untied me and presented me with a perfectly wrapped bundle of presents. A turquoise sundress that lightly covered nearly every inch of my body, matching sandals, sparkly earrings and a big beach hat.

He told me "Go take a shower and get ready to go out I want to show off my beautiful wife in the sunshine."

I did.

I did not speak a word of what I'd endured to anyone. The rest of the cruise was what you'd expect the honeymoon of two newlyweds deeply in love would look like. I convinced myself I must have misunderstood my husband and his actions in the first days of our marriage. I could not remember everything he'd done or in what order so I decided I completely over-reacted and I needed to check myself.

Hard science reveals what was really going on in my head. The abuse triggered my brain's protective mechanism. The brain stores traumatic memories differently than other types of memories. Tucks them away so the victim has a much harder time getting to them.

Our brains try to protect us. The brains of domestic violence and rape victims are in cahoots with the enemy.

The first time Travis strangled me was right after our one year anniversary party in our home after all of our

> **It takes 1/10th of a handshake to strangle a person.**

friends had gone. He held me against our living room wall by my throat and said only he could decide whether I would live or die. I was certain I was going to die.

When I came to, Travis wasn't there. I went to the powder-room to see what felt like a noose still tight around my neck. There wasn't a mark on me. Many years later I fled a classroom in tears after the professor explained that the pressure it takes to strangle someone is about one-tenth the amount of pressure a healthy male uses when giving a handshake. So little effort required to take another's life.

It's more common for people to say they were choked. But choking happens on the inside of the throat. Strangulation is when pressure is applied from the outside cutting off both air and blood supply.

Beyond putting me at death's door at the moment, Travis could still kill me. He's going to be in prison for many more years but the times he strangled me could still kill me. Could be today, could be ten years from now. Because being strangled damages the heart and lungs. One little blood clot comes loose and, BAM, the same result as a bullet to my brain from Travis' gun.

I'm a ticking time bomb and inside my head all of my springs and gears were deformed by the abuse, and the trauma, and the Post Traumatic Stress Disorder (PTSD).

Later, after I transitioned from victim to survivor I threw myself into learning exactly what trauma does to the brain and why the hell I stayed. I'd like to say I did it to save other women. I didn't. I was desperate to quiet my night terrors and the constant certainty I would be beaten again or killed at any moment of the day or night.

Once I earned my degree, I began my career as a victim's advocate with the intention of saving others. Soon I was traveling all over the U.S. sharing my experience and delivering training about domestic violence, sexual assault, how trauma re-wires the brain and how a trauma-informed, evidence-based, investigation and prosecution of Travis saved my life.

When Travis beat me he often put his hands around my throat. The neighbors would hear the ruckus and call the cops. Travis would be arrested. I'd bail him out and I'd go to the prosecutor's office to write out a statement that it was all a big understanding and really my fault for making Travis mad. While the criminal case plodded along Travis would cook, clean, bring me flowers and give me back-rubs along with a million apologies and a million promises of "never again".

> ## "A DV victim is in the most danger when they leave."

Because I was an uncooperative victim, prosecutors had no choice but to eventually dismiss the charges. Seven times we did this dance and once charges were dropped the back-rubs went away and the beatings started, again.

The next time, the last time, a police officer and a prosecutor teamed up to get a conviction without my cooperation.

Officer Brandt and Mary, the prosecutor, did what I could never do, they stopped Travis. They saved my life even as I looked for ways to get my husband back home.

> **"When Travis would start punching, kicking, raping and strangling me, it was never a surprise."**

The majority of people, even some victim advocates, will say "Why did she stay?! I'd just get out of there." Except you probably wouldn't. The vast majority of victims do not.

I stayed because if I physically left him I had no doubt he

would immediately kill me. I wasn't wrong, the odds were definitely not in my favor.

Statistically, a domestic violence victim is in the most danger when they leave the abuser.

There was a study where researchers interviewed a bunch of dudes who killed their wives and the trigger, according to the guys who went all the way, was the wife leaving or even saying she was going to leave.

All the arrests and charges before Brandt and Mary arrived in my life would inevitably lead me to the prosecutor's office asking that charges be dropped.

Even when Travis was in jail and I was in a secure room in the courthouse I could not believe I was safe from him. A domestic violence victim walks around with the feeling they're in mortal danger all the time. An advocate once told me "Sheryl, he is over there locked up in jail. You have some time to get to the shelter, get away from him, you can help us send him to prison this time. You're safe."

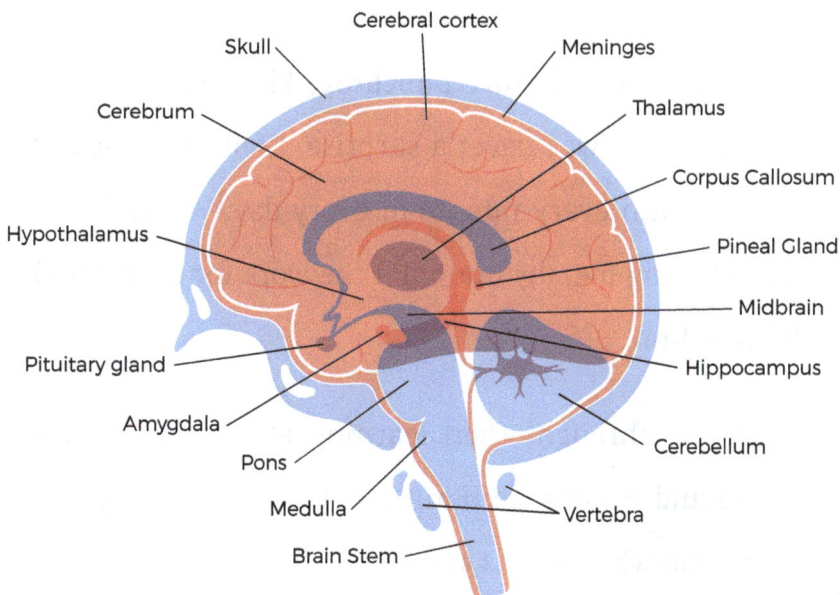

Cerebral cortex
Skull
Meninges
Cerebrum
Thalamus
Corpus Callosum
Hypothalamus
Pineal Gland
Midbrain
Pituitary gland
Hippocampus
Amygdala
Pons
Cerebellum
Medulla
Vertebra
Brain Stem

Those statements make perfect sense, unless you've experienced violent abuse at the hands of someone you love. Then those assurances feel like lies.

When you have been violently and repeatedly abused you've either gone completely numb and are unable to remember large chunks of the incidents or every cell in your body is screaming "HE'S GOING TO KILL YOU AND IT'S GOING TO HAPPEN RIGHT HERE, RIGHT NOW!"

When Travis would start punching, kicking, raping or strangling me it was never a surprise. I felt under attack and near death every minute of every day. When Travis wasn't abusing me, my brain did the work for him. And I still loved him.

From living through, then learning about, the effects of abuse and trauma on brain function I can give you a glimpse into why victims stay.

Violent crimes are a form of trauma. The incidents change the victim fundamentally. Trauma causes profound and lasting changes in brain function, memory, emotion and in the mind.

When under attack the victim's body dumps a load of pain-numbing endorphins into the system causing physiological collapse. Endorphins are those feel good chemicals. They reduce pain and make a body feel good.

Most people are familiar with the "runner's high" when an athlete is doing a pounding workout and endorphins are released making them able to push on, similar to a shot of morphine.

A flood of endorphins can cause a victim to freeze. Literally body functions slow down or stop.

Up there in our brain there's a gatekeeper called the thalamus, a cute little guy tucked right in the middle of our grey matter. Trauma punches a big hole in the floodgate that is the thalamus causing a flood of constant sensory overload. At the same time, all the work the thalamus does so we can pay attention, concentrate and learn new things... goes off-line.

Scientists have proven trauma literally changes a person at a genetic level. It changes the structure of chromosomes. That affects how genes function. Trauma creates a less resilient, more vulnerable, human being where a normally functioning, intelligent being used to be.

That's where I was the seventh time the neighbors called the cops because it sounded like Travis was battering down a wall. Using my head.

Officer Brandt and his partner pulled up and immediately called for an ambulance. As I left in the back of an ambulance Travis left in the back of a police car and was booked into jail.

> *Trauma literally changes a person at the genetic level.*

I needed some stitches and a small surgery to fix some of the lining of my throat. The strangulation cause veins to pop in my eyes (the medical term is petechiae) and bleeding in my throat. I couldn't speak at all for three days.

On the fourth day Officer Brandt came in to visit. Apparently, he asked the nurses to let him know as soon as I was able to talk.

He brought the county's prosecutor, Mary, who exclusively handled domestic violence cases

I immediately started in with accusations Brandt took everything out of context and drew the wrong conclusion and I was the one he should have arrested, not Travis. I told Mary I wouldn't testify against my husband and she couldn't make me.

Mary said "I'll never put you on the stand but we're sending him to prison."

> **Trauma Informed prosecution doesn't require a victim's testimony.**

I assumed at that point I was not actually awake and this was some sort of dream.

I grabbed the ice water from the hospital bedside table and stuck my whole hand in it. The shock of the cold water assured me I was definitely awake.

Mary explained that while still at the scene, Officer Brandt called her to explain the situation. I'd become quite the infamous victim in the local legal system. Yay, finally got my fame.

Mary told him exactly what to photograph, additional questions to ask witnesses and she contacted hospital staff while I was still on my ambulance ride to tell them which photographs she needed them to take of me and my visible wounds and documentation of every bit of damage inside and out, including x-rays that showed previous injuries that had since mostly healed.

I felt dead. I felt like I was dying. I was numb and I could barely remember my own name. Then I was seized with a terror I'd never experienced before. Panic attack, anxiety attack, my mouth went dry and my heart nearly beat out of my chest.

"I have got to go home right now!"

Officer Brandt called a nurse while Mary explained I did not need to go home I needed to get better. When I told her I had to get home because Travis would want me with him, Mary told something that changed the game forever.

Mary used the initial police and medical reports at Travis' initial arraignment to convince the judge he was too dangerous to be released on any amount of bond.

He couldn't get out. He couldn't get to me. I could not wrap my mind around it and all I could say was "How?" My brain refused to comprehend.

Mary explained to me about evidence based, trauma informed, investigation and prosecution.

Essentially, it allows all the facts in evidence to be presented in court along with law enforcement, witnesses and medical professionals' testimony, to show probably cause and eventually guilt. Even when the victim is unwilling or unable to testify.

In under five minutes these two professionals gave me my first glimpse into why the hell I stayed. They explained the arrest, the charges and any future convictions were not on me. In fact they had nothing to do with me… all of the legal wrangling was solely on them. Having no power over that situation flooded me with peace.

All the years of feeling responsible for everything bad that happened to me, immobile, unable to help myself out of misery had me carrying around a cumbersome, thick, shell and that day it developed the tiniest crack.

> *"He promised he would never hurt me again. He was right."*

I do not know what it was about Mary. She didn't pressure, she didn't try to talk sense into me, she never made me feel responsible for everything that happened in court and in my marriage. And parts of my brain and my very being began to awaken.

I felt more and more like my original self every day that Travis was in jail waiting for trial.

Marriage Doesn't Work

When I got home the jail calls from Travis were nearly constant. I found myself desperate to find a way to get him out of jail. Otherwise, I knew he'd kill me for not helping him.

Even if I had $10M cash on my kitchen counter right at that moment I still had no way of getting him out. But my trauma prevented that fact from grasping reality. To me he could still kill me at any time.

So I did what I could do to keep myself safe I assured him I loved him. I promised I was not going to ever testify against him, that I would wait for him to get out of jail.

He told me he loved me more than his own life. He apologized and promised he would never hurt me again in any way.

He was right.

The criminal case moved forward rather quickly because Travis was behind bars. Defendants who are roaming around free on bond are happy to have their defense

"The problem with marriage is you are bound to your abuser by law"

~ Random Fact

Marriage Doesn't Work

attorney stall their case for as long as possible. The ones who are locked up are far more interested in their right to a speedy trial.

Our church friends and even our pastor stood by Travis. Travis was the beautiful one, Travis had the charisma, Travis wrote the big donation checks and no one could imagine how I'd gone crazy enough to get myself cut off from all of that.

I'm not mad, I don't feel betrayed, and they are not bad people. Over the years I have come to understand people do not want their blinders removed. To believe I was a victim put them far too close to a violent criminal so they did not believe me. People generally prefer willful ignorance. They don't tune in to the commercial with all the abused dogs and cats, they turn the channel.

They turned the channel on me.

One day Mary called just to check on me and to let me know there would be a preliminary hearing but she was not going to subpoena me to testify. She said I had a right to know what was happening in the case. She did not even try to talk me into participating. Given my track record she probably expected I'd get on the stand and blow her entire case apart.

I'm sure she was right. If I'd been in the same room with Travis I would have absolutely said exactly what I knew he'd want me to say.

I thanked her, she asked if I was sleeping "You sound so tired." I told her Travis's repeated phone calls were keeping me from sleeping "I guess I'm on edge."

Mary said "Wait, he's calling you from jail?! The judge put a no-contact order in place so he's in violation. Give me an hour I'll call you back, try to take a nap, this is stopping right now."

Then Mary did something absolutely brilliant.

Always true to her word, Mary called back in :59 minutes and let me know Travis's phone privileges were suspended. He was cut off. For the first time in a long time, I believed the word of someone who was not Travis.

Not an hour later the phone rang, it was Travis. I was certain he'd be able to reach through the phone and strangle me with the cord. I listened to him threaten me and call me horrible names. I stayed on the line while he reminded me of things he'd done before and explicitly told me what he intended to do as soon as he got his hands on me, again.

I did not hang up. I couldn't hang up, I didn't want to make him even angrier. That was reasoning by my short-circuited, trauma-hijacked brain.

I stayed glued to the landline moving from numbness to terror to resignation that this was, and always would be my life.

Then my cell phone pinged, a number I didn't recognize.

> ## "He made my life miserable from his jail cell."

I opened the text "Sheryl, it's Mary. Travis is on the phone with you isn't he?"

I replied "Yes"

She sent "Hang in there, BRB."

It hurt that Mary, the person who I imagined might actually deliver me from hell wanted me to listen to more abuse and threats. I wasn't going to hang up, anyway. For some reason I wanted Mary to want me to.

And then the line went silent. Still, I stayed on the line, what if Travis was still there and he thought I hung up on him.

Then Mary texted again "Hang up, I'm calling you."

I looked between the text and the phone receiver with absolutely no idea what to do. I could not make a decision based on a simple instruction to put the phone in its cradle so I could receive Mary's call.

> **"** *12 years on eight charges* **"**

Then, my body took over where my brain froze and from muscle memory I just reached over and hung up the phone.

It rang immediately. It was Mary "Sheryl, I am so sorry I asked you to stay on the line longer. A jailer texted me that Travis was on the phone, he was using another inmates credentials to call you. When we realized what Travis was saying we wanted to get as much of it as possible on the recording. When he stopped making admissions and turned back to straight name calling we cut him off. Also, he not only confessed but I'm adding charges for threatening by electronic device and intimidating a witness."

I was completely speechless.

Mary sounded worried "Sheryl, hey girl, are you there?"

I was nodding yes vigorously but that was no help to Mary "Sheryl, please answer me."

I croaked out a "Yes".

I was completely distracted by a feeling in my chest. Below my heart but above my belly. It was warm, pleasantly warm and it began growing and spreading through my chest and into my limbs. I did not recognize it at first. It had been so long. Then, I was able to give it a name. It was hope.

That night I slept without night terrors. I slept and when I woke up I did not feel tired. The bad times still rolled in on a regular basis but that morning I had hope that I might not only survive my victimization, but that I might be just fine.

There was no trial. Travis's attorney listened to the recorded jail call and strongly encouraged Travis to take any deal the prosecutor was willing to offer. It was a bad deal for Travis but still a lighter sentence than a jury was likely to hand out after seeing the gruesome photos of my injuries and listening to his tell-all call to me.

12 years on a total of eight criminal charges.

Mary introduced me to a friend with whom she'd gone to law school. Amy worked for legal aid and she helped me file for divorce and all that followed. A federal grant earmarked for services to help victims of crime paid Amy's salary so she did all of my legal work at no charge to me.

My divorce was just as messy and drawn out as most divorces are. Travis had no intention of losing the bit of control he still held over my head.

You'd think divorcing a convicted felon who is serving prison time would be simple. Of course it didn't work out that way. Thanks to lots of donations to his unofficial "Free Travis" fund at the church my husband had plenty of time and money to hire two attorneys and make my life somewhat miserable from his prison cell on the other side of the state.

I nearly gave up on getting a divorce a few times along with way. What did it matter?

> **"Victims of crime are best served through trauma informed therapy."**

"It matters." said Amy. She was right. I was tied and bound to him. Even though he couldn't get to me he still had his hands around my neck.

"This is the problem with marriage, you are bound to your partner by law, and even if you wanted to get out, you can't. And when you try, it becomes complete legal hell to even try."

Then Amy came up with a brilliant plan to divert some of Travis and his attorneys attention while creating a possible tool to use in the divorce war.

Amy helped me file a protective order against Travis. It did not look hopeful. The judge could not see how I could need a protective order when my abuser was in prison and would stay there for quite a while. Amy's legal arguments finally prevailed and because Travis was convicted of multiple felonies against me the judge was able to grant a lifetime protective order.

That finding encouraged the divorce judge to speed things along. If there's a court order that Travis cannot so much as call me, what would be the basis of keeping the marriage intact? The fact he was in prison for violently abusing me over a number of years was apparently not sufficient grounds for divorce. What a crock, but it was finally done.

I mourned the death of my marriage. It brought on strong PTSD symptoms. I couldn't sleep. I couldn't eat. I constantly felt cold. I'd been changed for the worse and permanently. I didn't even feel like a person anymore, I had no future I could envision.

I startled at every noise. I had nightmares about my abuse when I slept and flashbacks when I was awake.

The church had been the center of my spiritual and social life and I was effectively banished from there. So much for Christian love.

A professor in one of my classes noticed my attendance and grades were both dropping. She pulled me aside and asked if I needed some help. I dissolved into tears as I gave her a recap of what I had been through and the fact I really was not worthy of the time and space I took up in her class.

She cried with me then she asked if she could make a suggestion. I had nowhere to go and no desire to do anything, so I was open to suggestions.

She gave me the contact information for a colleague who is a trauma-informed psychologist.

I'd never held people who poke around other people's heads in very high esteem. I grew up believing that whining about your problems to someone else is weak. A character trait that served Travis very well.

But I gave Miranda a shot. By the end of the first appointment that warmth had returned. I felt and glimpsed hope, again.

> *He was the hunter I was the prey.*

Miranda explained that victims of crime are best served through trauma-informed therapy. I was not going to talk over and over about the things Travis did to me. Miranda says that is a form of re-victimization and can actually block healing.

Instead she took on the role of teacher for me. I learned about the impact of stressful events mentally, physically, short and long term. I learned coping skills specific to the crimes committed against me. I learned how to regulate the way I interpreted situations and interactions. Eventually I also learned how to control my reactions to memories, flashbacks, panic attacks and then, I was able to mostly keep Travis out of my dreams.

I don't date. I will never get married again. Miranda says I may change my mind eventually. That's the one and only

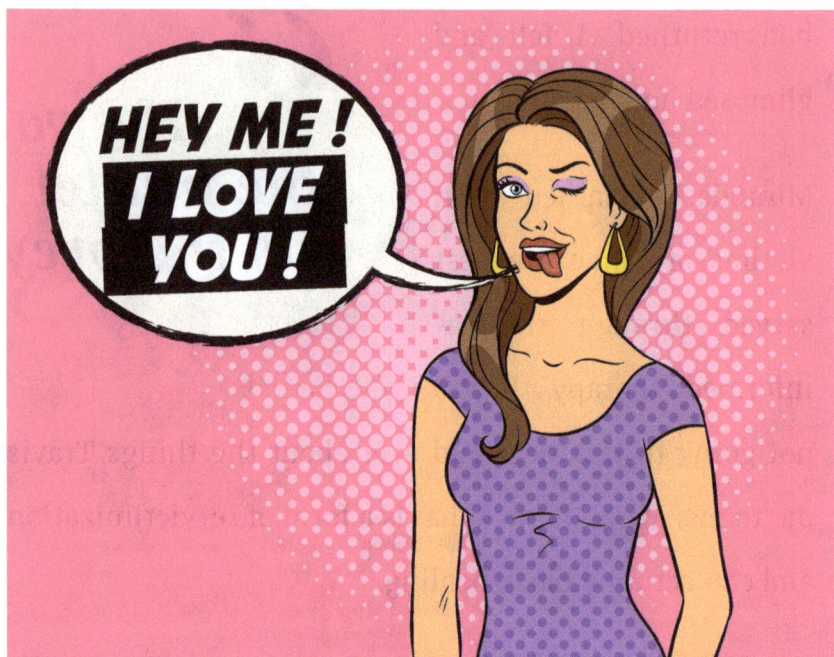

place Miranda is wrong. I will never trust myself where a romantic relationship is concerned. I didn't see a single, red, flag until I was tied to a bed on a boat sailing away from my former life and solid ground.

I can say that I have recently found happiness and peace. And my warm hope continues to grow inside my belly.

I now understand that falling for Travis was not a sin or a failure on my part. He was the hunter and I was the prey. He was a master manipulator and I was an open and honest person.

I've regained at least parts of my life and personality that Travis had wiped away.

I love my work. I get to help women move from being victims to becoming survivors. I get to train members of law enforcement, other advocates and social workers on using a trauma-informed approach in any case involving a victim of crime.

I will never know if a woman was able to successfully leave an abusive situation because of me. I'll certainly never know if my intervention kept someone from being further victimized or murdered.

What I do know is I have hope. It is warm and it is growing.

And sharing that hope might prevent someone else from becoming victimized or dead.

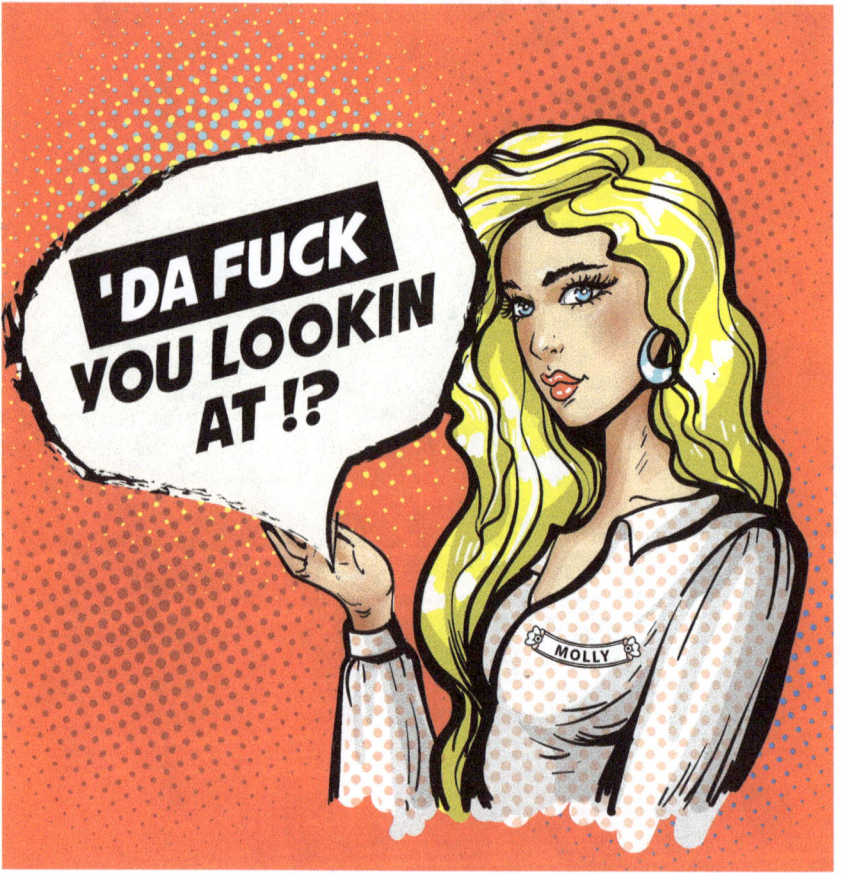

Marriage Doesn't Work

The Condom Broke... My Marriage

"We have the same relationship struggles as straight people."

~Baldrik KrappeSchwänze, Random Ghost Author

I was running. I'd accidentally left my wallet in the car. So I jogged back, grabbed my wallet and was now trying to catch up with my friends before anything amazing happened without me.

As I looked for my glimmer; that's what we call our group... a glimmer. We're basically a group of unicorns. Mystical and horny.

I was scanning the crowds when I was distracted by a beautiful shirtless buff boy in very tiny shorts, boots and nothing else. Mmmmm, mmmmm, MMMMM

"Yass honey!" I shouted.

When my head swiveled back in the direction in which I was traveling, forward never straight of course, I found myself staring into the most beautiful blue eyes I'd ever seen. Thick, dark, lashes highlighting the color and just the right amount of guy-liner to set the whole look ablaze.

That's how I met Dale on that hot, July, day in Dallas, 2008. LGBTQA Pride celebrations were in full swing and swish.

Every bit of the LGBTQA alphabet was represented by the hundreds, probably thousands. If you need a translator LGBTQA stands for: Lesbian, gay, bisexual, transgender, questioning and ally.

My first word to my future love, and the man who would shatter my heart, was "David".

"No, Dale." He replied "Have we met?"

"No, sorry, I'm David. And you're Dale."

We were grinning like idiots, I'm sure. We chatted about what a glorious day it was for Pride celebrations. Shared a mostly brotherly hug to celebrate living out of the closet, showing our Pride mostly without fear. Soon we agreed to find my glimmer and all go to the Pride Parade together.

Throughout the afternoon we quickly covered the litany of questions gay boys usually chat about on a first date.

My I.T. job for a small Home Décor business and my love of my part-time gig as a writer/director at the local community theater.

Dale was a waiter at a locally owned, high end, restaurant. Over time it became glaringly clear he had a love of his part-time hobby, getting on the dicks of guys who were not me. He didn't disclose that particular hobby at the time.

Throughout the afternoon we also enjoyed a cocktail with the group pretty much wherever the opportunity presented itself.

We smoothly glided into the "when did you come out?" stories.

> **"Glimmer, thats what we called our group."**

This is always a starting point on a first date between homosexuals. And our random run-in quickly turned into our first date.

The coming out story is a mutual touchstone and unless still closeted, an experience every gay man shares. The rest of the alphabet, too. I'm not throwing shade I just don't know the experience firsthand of those who are lesbian, trans, bi, questioning or non-binary.

I can send love and support to them all I just don't understand it from a place inside my own experiences.

Some gay coming out stories are heartwarming, some heart breaking.

Regardless of the individual experience it is a common thread woven through the entire non-straight community. As Ellen DeGeneres would say while shaking her head "Ohhhhh, straight people."

> **He did not disclose to me his part-time hobby.**

Whether cisgender and straight, you know, their whole lives they feel the junk they were born with indeed aligns with the sex they believe they are. Eggplant, boy. Taco, girl. Live your life.

Or the heterosexuals, the straight folk, the breeders.

They never had to have "the talk".

Which of you reading this who love the opposite sex had to sit your parents down, palms sweating, heart racing, fear and anxiety running rampant to say "Mom, Dad, I'm straight."

It's one of the things that makes us next level. The struggle is really real.

How and when we come out, then how friends and family react to the fact, is something every newly smitten kitten can relate to and share.

Plus, you get a decent overview of your new boy, his family, friends and past damage. It ramps up the intimacy pretty quickly.

The glimmer took to Dale almost as quickly as I did. Sort of unusual for a group of alpha prima donna bitchy queens. Dale could give as well as he could take. That, too, became glaringly obvious over time. But for the day we were enjoying making new friends in a safe space where we could be authentic. We celebrated what Lady GaGa sings for us because we were born this way, baby. People are honestly born gay or straight or something else. It's not a choice, do not even come at me with some pray the gay out bullshit. Love is love is love. I know because I lived it.

The one exception to the bitchy, and also absolutely fantastic, gay queens in our glimmer is Molly. Molly is a true ally. The A+ in our LGBTQA friend groups.

She is the incredibly hot, wickedly funny, matriarch and fruit fly of the group.

Not that Molly is much older than us, she's younger than some but she has amazing maternal instincts where the members of the glimmer are involved. Especially towards those who were turned out and disowned by a parent when they came out as gay.

If you're not familiar a "fruit fly" refers to a female friend who is hot, supports equality as a vocal ally and is not in love with a gay boy. She's a little fruit fly buzzing about

> ## *It's one of the things that makes us next level.*

happily.

Fag hags are those unfortunate souls who hold on to unrequited love for a gay man for so long they forget to even look for a straight match.

Maybe they are actually the most fortunate of us all. No marriage, no divorce. There is still bitter heartache.

Apparently no matter what you do, or don't do, most everyone will experience bitter heartache before sliding feet first into their grave.

Molly is nowhere near the end of her existence. When you're with her you feel more alive.

She is also an important accessory for every member of the glimmer.

How hot a gay boy is, is a direct correlation to how hot his straight girlfriend is.

> **"A fruit fly refers to a female friend who is hot."**

Sounds harsh but I didn't make the rules, it's just true. We hit the jackpot with Molly and we all love her dearly.

She is brilliant, well-spoken, classy, has at least 50 pairs of designer shoes and swears like a sailor.

Molly was blessed with gorgeous green eyes that turn blue-grey if provoked. I tell you she has gorgeous, wavy, red hair to explain just how she can accelerate from zero to scary bitch in under ten seconds if someone she loves is wronged. We say her eyes and hair are warning labels, woe to anyone who misses the signs. She can snatch a bitch up short real quick if they cross a line. Of course this glimmer of bitchy queens views her as our personal goddess.

She can also drink any of us under the table.

The Pride Parade would start in thirty minutes.

We'd secured a primo table on the patio of a bistro along the parade route. The cocktails, laughter, and ever longer lingering hugs continued all through the early evening. The summer sun just giving way to some shade on the parade route.

That's when Dale and I went there.

> **" *Fag hags hold on to love for a gay man.* "**

In the family, all of us who are somehow queer compared to heterosexuals, are considered family. The greater gay family refer to what Dale and I did next as dropping the ex-boyfriend bomb.

Sometimes it's just a slip and can indicate the potential suitor isn't quite out of, or over, the last relationship.

Sometimes you drop the name and former relationship status to show you've been in a committed relationship before. And while that one did not work out you remain a viable potential partner. To be blunt, you're signaling you are not just looking for an endless string of guys on Grindr for hook-ups with a large number of mainly strangers.

> **" How hot a gay boy is, is in direct connection to how hot his straight girlfriend is. "**

You want true love.

You can learn a lot about a person, of any sexual orientation, by how they tell the tale of past love, life and break-up.

Inevitably discussion of an ex leads to the "why did you break up?" question.

There are those who trash their ex so harshly and so often you begin thinking of how they'll trash talk about you to anyone who will listen when the relationship fails. Or even during the relationship. It's not an attractive look on anyone.

You can tell some are still holding on to the ex and the love. Making moves to date and mate, only just barely going through the motions. It's sad. Some are drawn to those people, believing they can re-channel that love to themselves. It rarely works that way, though.

You have the guys who describe themselves as being separated from their longtime partner. What they really mean is their partner did not come with them this evening and they've been "separated" since parting ways at their mutual home this morning.

To me the most attractive matches are those who speak of their exes as friends. It was love, it broke, they came out the other side and still care about each other. Isn't that what we all want in our lives? If things get broken they can be mended without leaving a trail of fiery rubble in each other's lives.

That is how Dale described his ex and seemed ready to move along to another topic of conversation. Fine by me, it's dreadfully annoying when someone won't shut UP about their ex. Moving along.

I hadn't had a partner in years, I was friendly with exes. Molly says I'm too particular. I prefer to think of it as refusing to settle for anything less than butterflies.

Those beautiful winged creatures were flitting around my stomach at that moment like a tiny tornado.

Then Dale, looking into my eyes, took my hand and leaned forward. And I leaned forward and it happened. Our first kiss. As the Pride Parade passed by. We kissed right between the float topped with drag queens on poles and the PFLAG float.

IT.WAS.EVERYTHING.

" *You learn a lot about a person by how they tell the tale of their last love* "

~ *Random Fact*

Marriage Doesn't Work

Things just sped up from there. And we already had the gas pedal firmly pressed to the floor.

We barreled into love. We were Facebook official in the blink of an eye.

> **We broke lesbian couple's speed record for moving in together.**

There's a joke, what do lesbians do on a second date? They rent a U-Haul.

We may have broken any lesbian couple's land speed record for moving in together.

Dale joined me in my 3,000 square foot loft with a view.

My gayborhood is close knit. Solidly upper middle class, educated, well-groomed and always up for a cocktail. Or four. Although I'd never been a heavy drinker it was fun feeling like you're living in the midst of an epic cocktail party.

The community was good for the relationship. Living free range amongst only breeders can cause a type of minority stress. Researchers have found minority stress is triggered by experiences unique to that minority. In our case: Gay. It's common for gay men to experience one or more instances of harassment, discrimination, micro-aggression and even violent forms of gay bashing.

Been there, done that, got the hospital bills. That was all behind me, now.

Dale and I lived, and loved, in a cocoon. Our lives melding seamlessly into joint checking and credit card accounts, shared household bills, belongings and friends.

Dale didn't seem to have any close friends but that was fine, the glimmer could only reach a certain size before some would have to break off into just a regular sprinkling of glitter.

Had we given it more thought, we might have realized the obvious. There was a big reason Dale didn't have friends.

But he'd dazzled us and he was in.

Gay marriage was still illegal then but we yearned to make our union official. This was 2008. The funny thing about how long it took to be granted the right to wed is, as it turns out same-sex couples do marriage better than heterosexual couples. I am not kidding, research has been done. There are facts and graphs and everything!

Research out of UCLA shows, and I quote "first-wave gay marriages have proved more durable than straight ones."

> **First wave gay marriages proved more durable than straight ones.**

Add to that the finding that same-sex couples who are allowed to legally form a romantic union are more likely to stay in a committed relationship than those not allowed the right to marry.

> **"** *Its common for gay people to experience harrassment, discrimination, micro-aggression and violence* **"**

~ *Random Fact*

All those right wing Christians squawking about "It's Adam and Eve not Adam and Steve!" need to slow their roll. As it turns out gay marriage seems to be TOTES (totally) God's will.

But in 2008 Dale and I were denied the right.

So we looked into my Scottish heritage and decided on a handfasting ceremony to bind us together, further.

Handfasting is a Celtic tradition. A couple professing their love for each other with at least two witnesses present was legally binding. Though the Scots considered it a temporary marriage. Like a place holder for next year's real church ceremony. Our coupling was quite a bit more temporary than I imagined.

But the day of our union was glorious.

We held the ceremony in one of the theater spaces where I direct plays.

And it was a production befitting a gaggle of gorgeous

gays plus Molly.

We wrote our own vows, we held each other's right hands as Molly wrapped a red ribbon around them. We took each other as husband. We kissed, friends cheered then we had one hell of a party.

> " *It was a production befitting a gaggle of gorgeous gays plus Molly.* "

I'll admit it. Part of the magic of having a handfasting to bind us one to the other wasn't rooted in our love and commitment to each other. That was part of it.

We also wanted to publicly declare we were ONE in our love. That our love was equal to anyone else's. The fact gay marriage was still forbidden certainly added a spark to the endeavor. Plus we felt like trailblazing pioneers clearing the way to married bliss for all.

Marriage Doesn't Work

It came to pass, just up the street from where we were kinda-gay-marrying, Sir Elton John was in concert with Billy Joel.

Which drew that hate monger Fred Phelps and a lot of his knuckle-dragging Westboro Baptist Church congregation.

They were camped up the street protesting with their handmade "God Hates Fags" signs because a gay guy was playing the piano and singing. Unbeknownst to their pea brains born of a very shallow gene pool, just a few blocks away two gay guys were binding themselves and their lives together as husband and husband.

The irony was one of our greatest wedding gifts.

The second came when magnificent Molly insisted on loft-sitting for us with her hunk of a boyfriend while we honeymooned in Key West.

We stayed in a little B&B with a private pool perfect for skinny dipping and within walking distance of Higgs Beach, Duvall Street, and about 100 bars. Key West is uber gay friendly, and we frequented only the gayest of the gay.

We were basking in the sunshine and our love.

Meanwhile back home Molly decided to give the loft a thorough cleaning. The whirlwind of wedding and honeymoon preparations left the homestead in dire need of a good tidy up and airing out.

Things were certainly about to be outed.

Molly and her beau decided to document how two, gay, men were living in squalor and it took a straight couple to restore order.

They took before and after pictures.

Upon returning home to our sparkling clean loft and a bottle of Veuve Cliquot champagne waiting on ice greeted us.

We marveled, toasted, sipped, then we found Molly's note.

"Welcome home my little lovebirds! Brad and I whipped this place into shape while you were whooping it up in Key West. We made you a little virtual photo album of the before and after photos! Enjoy the laughs!"

And there was a website link and a password.

Molly made absolutely everything better. At least that was always her intention.

As we clicked through the before and after photos we laughed, we vowed to never allow another human being to know how disorganized and dirty we'd allowed our loft to become. We also vowed to buy Molly's drinks for several months, at least.

> ❝ *Molly had taken a picture...in the foreground was clearly a used condom.* ❞

I clicked the right arrow, again, and there with our bed in

the background of the shot Molly had taken a picture of what she found under the bed.

Dangling from the end of a letter opener in the foreground was clearly a used condom. Obviously Molly thought it would be hilarious to point out a slightly embarrassing sign of our passion.

Dale stared. I stared. A used condom what in the actual fuck?

I turned slowly to look into Dale's beautiful blue eyes with tears in mine. You see, Dale and I did not use condoms when we made love. We were both negative for an array of STD's including AIDS so we went bareback.

I returned to staring at the picture and I went numb. Dale began babbling excuses and trying to close the web page and begging forgiveness. I felt a whole, lot, of nothing.

I stood up, grabbed my phone, keys, and wallet. The same wallet that brought Dale and I together on that Sunny Pride Saturday.

And I left.

I left my home, I left my husband, I left my life in a pool of betrayal and went straight to Molly's.

I did not leave her guestroom for a week. Molly and Brad did their best but my heart was shattered into a million black pieces and there were times I thought I'd actually died and was in hell.

It was during that time Molly, Brad and some of the larger members of the glimmer went to my loft and invited Dale to be gone, immediately.

He is a cheat but he's no idiot. He gathered a few things and left. No emotion, head down and he left.

He left my loft, he left me, and he left the marriage without another word.

Not a call.

Not a letter.

Not a text.

Not an email.

Just gone.

I guess he must have gone to whoever that condom came off of in my bed just before our wedding. Or to one of the others. Or to someone new. I honestly no longer care.

> *No emotion, head down, he just left.*

I believed I'd found "the one". Dale was my forever someone. Certain we could rely on each other and enjoy the absolute certainty we were always beside the person we could trust the most in our lives. For the rest of our lives.

Then, the condom broke my marriage.

Unraveling our love union was much easier than dividing our finances and belongings.

Marriage Doesn't Work

No legitimate wedding means no divorce. We were left with essentially the same rights as a landlord -tenant relationship.

Unable to end the union in divorce court, Dale and I dragged each other through multiple civil suits communicating only through court filings and civil attorneys.

That all ended the same way it does for most straight, gay, or lesbian couples who marry then divorce these days ... we both came out poorer and angrier. Yay equality!

> **"Marriage ruined my life, I will never love romantically again."**

I've never dated, again. I'll enjoy some carnal knowledge with a beautiful guy from time-to-time. I'm not made of stone!

But Dale was my ruin. My love life is over.

That was all twelve years ago I feel quite confident in saying I will never love romantically, again.

My glimmer surrounds me. They saved me. They propped me up and kept me moving through life and work until I found the will and desire to make my triumphant return to real life.

They were all as blindsided as I was by Dale's cheating.

I got sober in AA. I started going to meetings because I was regularly drinking to the point of blacking out then waking to the fresh heartbreak of realizing Dale was gone. Which made me want to drink.

What I learned by working the program was that alcohol was Dale's way of distracting me. Keeping me slightly buzzed and completely unaware of how many men he'd had directly under my nose.

And that was some Ninja level adultery to pull off in our little "know your neighbor" gayborhood.

At least they used condoms, right? Ha!

I do have a sense of humor about it, 12 years later. It sounds like a trashy romance novel turned tragic.

I can no longer say I am friendly with all of my exes.

That's one reason I don't date. I don't want to be "that" guy always going on about how wronged and damaged I am. Boring and frankly beneath me.

I do not know what became of Dale. I know straight people think every gay person knows every other gay person but that's not the case.

I'm actually doing well. I can say I am happy, again.

A year after Dale split, I was honored to be Molly's Matron of Honor in her wedding to Brad.

Since then the couple has produced two of the most ridiculously gorgeous and brilliant children, ever. I might be slightly biased. I am, after all, their Fairy Godfather. I am part of their family and we have more than enough love to go around.

I haven't given up on gay marriage. For others. I'm glad for friends who have married their longtime partners in recent years. It seems like only a moment ago in history when LGBTQ couples were denied the right to bond in marriage. And, like me, had no way to undo any bond they'd knit together through divorce.

I am glad there's been some time for researchers to learn some things no one really expected about gay versus straight marriages.

> " *Same-sex couples have longer lasting relationships than their straight counterparts.* "

Straight people, especially straight men, think "gay" simply means fuck whatever catches your eye, whenever you want, then repeat. Ohhhhhh, straight people.

Research shows something

Marriage Doesn't Work

quite different. Research shows same-sex couples have longer lasting partnerships that their straight counterparts. On top of that, one study out of the University of Washington reveals

> **"** *Even though we couldn't get legally married, we still had to go through divorce.* **"**

same-sex couples get along better than hetero couples. It seems males and females bound in straight matrimony experience higher levels of trauma due to their squabbling than homosexual couples do.

It could be same-sex couples share a far more similar communication style and life experiences than straight folk.

It could be we really are next level and about as magical as a glimmer of unicorns.

I think it's important to understand from my story that

because even though we couldn't get married we formed a "marriage like" relationship and that failed and we went through a divorce type experience, using lawyers and courts, draining everything out of us including money, and that didn't work, either. Gay marriage seems to last longer than straight but at the end of the day it doesn't really work for anyone who gets married/divorced.

The story is two guys who fall in love and go down in flames. The info on gay marriage being stronger than straight is an interesting fact that people don't know. For these two characters; however, their marriage fell apart and the divorce/civil suits left them both damaged and pissed.

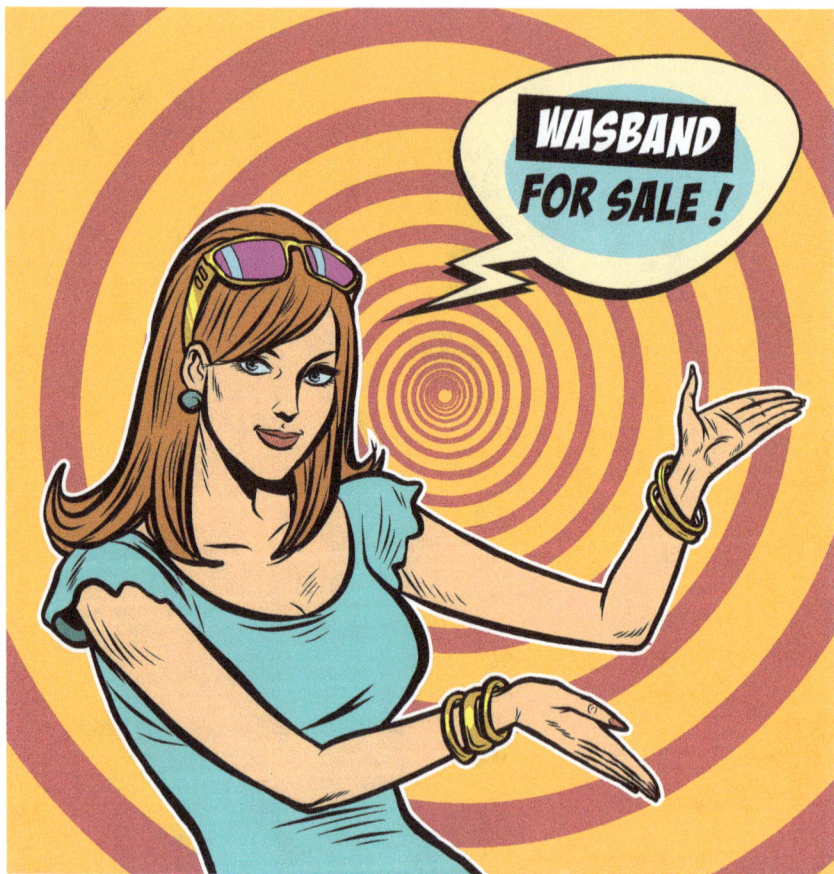

Marriage Doesn't Work

My Wasband

"Don't wait to have children."

~Molly Von SchwetzenKuchen, Random Ghost Author

◇◇◇◇◇◇◇◇◇◇◇◇◇◇◇◇◇◇◇◇◇◇◇◇◇◇◇◇◇◇◇◇◇◇◇◇

WARNING: Foul and Funny as Shit Language

◇◇◇◇◇◇◇◇◇◇◇◇◇◇◇◇◇◇◇◇◇◇◇◇◇◇◇◇◇◇◇◇◇◇◇◇

Hi, I'm Jane1. This is my #WASband story. It was love at first sight. Then the engagement, followed by 17 years of helliage before it went down in flames of infidelity. And when I say that please believe me when I tell you, I've mellowed out a lot in the heavenly 13 years since the divorce from Dickpimple. I'm not even bitter about the twatwaffle Jane2 anymore.

Of course in the beginning of our relationship it was magical. We were only half joking when we'd tell people it was an arranged marriage, because it was.

My Aunt and his father decided we should be together and neither of them is a person you want to disappoint, unless you want to continue hearing about it for a couple of decades. I was still in the womb when all of these preparations were being made. Surprisingly, when we became of age, We fell in love. We truly were in young love.

> **" *It was an arranged, yet deranged marriage* "**

I'd never wanted children, until I met Dickpimple. I wasn't even sure I would ever marry, until I met Dickpimple, my future WASband. WASband is what I call him when he manages to remove his head at least partially out of his

Marriage Doesn't Work

own ass. The rest of the time, which is most of the time, I refer to him simply as the sperm-donor, sometimes I throw in more colorful nicknames strictly for my own amusement.

It seemed like a love story fit for Shakespeare's "Anthony and Cleopatra". Our "Salad days", young, in love, inexperienced and carefree. We had the big church wedding complete with hideous brides' maids dresses. I really do need to send my bridesmaids a note of apology for those dresses they had to wear. I feel like we need a scientific study of what causes that

> **" Just have children, you will get divorced anyway. "**

phenomenon. Why does the soon-to-be bride pick out the fugliest bridesmaids dresses for her dearest friends and family to wear on her big day? And the kicker is, she truly believes with all of her heart "You'll be able to wear it again!" It's like some form of temporary blindness or a strange clothing dysmorphia that disappears as soon as the wedding photos arrive. It's a BIG RED FLAG that you're going into something you shouldn't be. Love may be blind, but so is the bride picking out bridesmaids' dresses. Blind and stupid. You can add Wedding Dresses and Bridesmaid dresses to the list of the world's biggest scams.

He wanted to get pregnant on the honeymoon. I did not want my children to be children of divorce like me, so I wanted to wait. I would say "Let's make sure our marriage and union is on firm footing before bringing children into the mix." Thinking back, why wait? This hesitation on my part should have been a foreboding warning about that Elephant in the room. 18 months after our second baby was born, we were divorced.

Dickpimple went through his little post-divorce crisis with a handful of 20 year old's. One day I was at his house and I opened the fridge to get the kids' juice boxes and there was a bottle of White Zinfandel. Seriously, dude, just ply her with Boone's Farm and be done with it. Skip forward to present day in the midst of COVID and geopolitical unrest. You could say everyone is a teensy bit on edge.

Now he's in the midst of divorce number two. Meet Jane2.

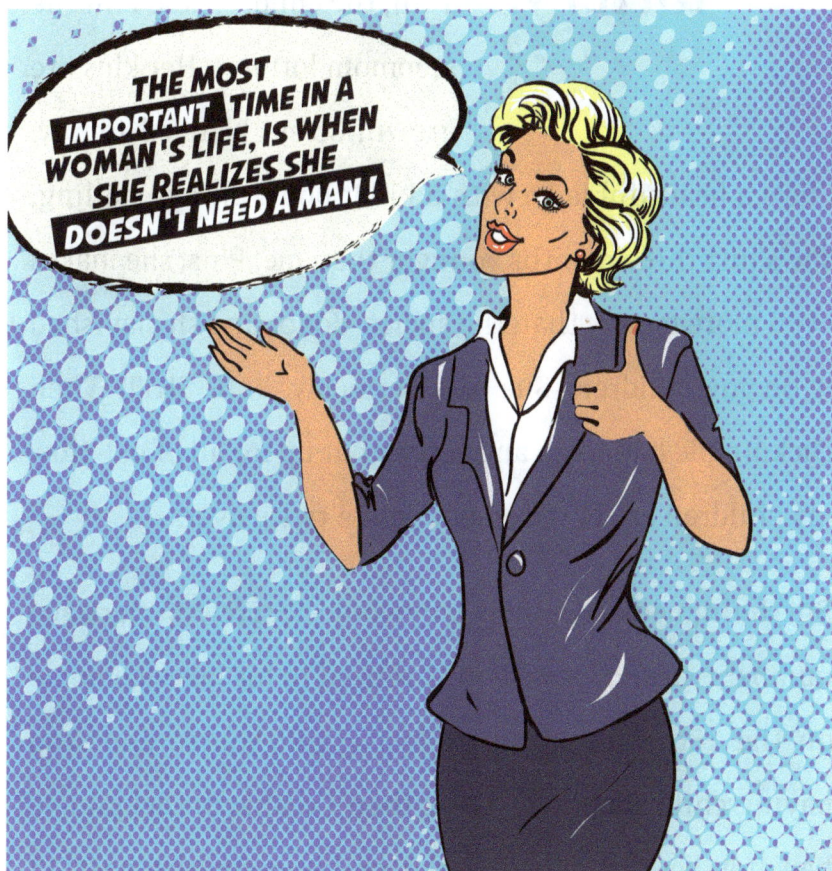

> ## " *The children and I hit the stepmom lottery.* "

After a time, pencil-dick got off the 20 year olds and found a second brilliant, smoking hot, wife. You're going to absolutely love Jane2.

Y'all, the children and I hit the stepmom lottery! Her kids are grown, so no blended family. She's a beautiful lady, with a killer body, always smiling, she's just three months younger than me. Plus, she makes even more money than the sperm-donor and she lavished it on my children. She was seriously, THE SHIT. Then Dickpimple had to go and screw that up for all of us! Now my children are children of divorce twice over.

But the immediate point is, why would he screw up marriage number two and immediately retreat to his lakeside home on the 18th hole of an exclusive golf course and stop paying child support? It was then I realized, Dickpimple had not been supporting the children for the past 12 years. That was ALL Jane2. I've known for several years that while Dickpimple desperately wanted children, he

> ## *It's never amicable.*

clearly wants nothing to do with raising them.

For months I had my children right around 98% of the time. Paying for all the food, clothing, shoes and utilities that come with that arrangement. I was trying to give Dickpimple and Jane2 time to sort things out, hoping he'd somehow manage to win her back and keep her in our lives, but that was not to be. It was too late.

The child support amount Dickpimple began withholding was a whopping $200 per month for our two children. Cheapest kiddie rent in the history of EVER said EVERYONE. Considering he makes around $300,000 a year. No one can understand why I took such a tiny amount of money in the divorce. I baffle friends, family and divorce attorneys. Here's the thing, in the divorce I just wanted OUT with my kids to get on with our lives. I didn't care that I was getting screwed. I cared about the children. He cared about the money so that seemed to me to be the straightest path to freedom.

I ignorantly believed him the day we stood in a parking lot, on a break from the court ordered co-parenting classes when he hugged me and said, "If you or the kids every need anything, I'll be there." But the moment wife number two gets the knives out he decides he no longer cares to support his children. Even when you both feel good about it, don't let your defenses down. I went 50 shades of Mama Bear, I filed a motion to modify custody and child support.

> **"When he saw I was completely over him, it drove him crazy."**

I got 100% custody and six times the amount of child support he'd been paying. Thankfully, because this child rearin' business is fucking expensive. And, being a complete idiot turned out to be a lot more expensive for mushroom-cap nipple-dick.

The benefit of this painful journey is I've gained a sense

> **"That's all the divorce revenge you'll ever need."**

of experience, strength and hope. Let me share some pro tips, tricks and tactics with you my friend. I Believe I have the experience to know what works, but more importantly, what you should and shouldn't do. You need to first wrap your mind around the fact that marriage and divorce are a marathon, not a sprint. Unless you're one of those young couples who marry and divorce within days or weeks. That is just a crazy sprint into madness and frankly it doesn't count.

I played the long game. I was perfectly willing to let him move on with his new life and new wife. What I wasn't willing to do was allow him to abandon his children. My dad did it to me, and it ain't happening again this time.

So, the first thing I did after the divorce was lose a bunch of weight and became HOT AGAIN! STAY HOT FOREVER. In my case I felt revenge was best served hot - you'll never get to be with this ever again Dickpimple fuck brain!

Then I went tits-up balls-out cougar on this hot, out-of-work, actor who rode a Harley and bar-tended part time.

> ## *His new ex-wife and housekeeper became my secret weapons.*

He was doing me full time whenever the kids went to their dad. After being with WASband for 18 years I couldn't get enough of a new man who was so in awe of my beauty, my brain, my body. He didn't have a paunch or a bald spot. I hadn't felt like that in, well, probably EVER. And while that's sad it's not terminal. It can be fixed. Bed the hot 20-something guy.

It was all fun and games and until, one weekend, I suddenly decided it was inevitable that I was to have a

Marriage Doesn't Work

complete breakdown over the break-up of my marriage to DICKpimple. So, I turned down all plans the next weekend the kids would be with the WASband and I readied myself for tragedy. I gathered the tissues, the candles, the incense, the girl toys, the playgirls, the blankets, the comfort food, a nice single malt scotch... and... "Sleepless in Seattle".

Then this really weird thing happened. Instead of a crying and screaming accompanied with jag, I was overcome with such a sense of peace and relief. I realized in that moment I was so much lonelier in our marital home with Dickpimple than I ever was all alone in my new house. In fact, I wasn't lonely at all, I was happy.

When Dickpimple could clearly see I was happy, completely over him and loving my new life it drove him absolutely crazy. I just kept smiling, while in my head I imagined repeatedly saluting him with both of my middle fingers. That's all the divorce revenge you'll ever need.

Then things took a very interesting turn. It came to

" *Women end up with the lions share after a Divorce* "

~ Random Fact

Marriage Doesn't Work

pass that his soon-to-be second ex-wife, Jane2, and our housekeeper became my secret weapon, my posse, his kryptonite. Hear me when I tell you Always, ALWAYS, hire the same cleaning lady as your ex. Trust me on this one. The beginning of divorce number two ended up being our golden ticket. Not for him, for the kids and me. He was playing the victim card to me claiming Jane2 kicked him out and that's why he was living at the lake. He must have been hit in the head with a golf ball because he had it exactly backwards. It was his choice to move to the lake home to party full-time. I know this because unbeknownst to him, his soon-to-be-ex, Jane2, started dishing over to me and offered to testify under oath to "the whole dirty truth, and nothing but the dirty truth".

> **" We wondered if he and his new roommate were sharing the same Rubber Ducky. "**

Seems Jane2 became grumpy when ol' Dickpimple picked up quite the compulsion for smoking pot every waking moment, spending a lot of time and money at the country club bar and frequenting hook-up apps. So gross. So Jane2 did what any sister would do, she began sending me, Jane1, a steady stream of screenshots of text messages between she and Dickpimple. You know the ones. The screenshots where she warned him more than once that his behavior was going to cost him custody of his kids if not result in prison time. The screenshots where she offered multiple times for him to come take back his marital home she moved into, for the good of his relationship with his children, which he... declined. The screenshots where she told him his excessive marijuana and alcohol use made him withdraw from everything and everyone while becoming completely emotionally unavailable to his wife and children.

Jane2 sent me monthly statements for that fancy golf club membership and the lake house to the tune of $1,000 per month. Keep in mind, this is at the same moment in time he's refusing to pay $200/month in child support to me. There were screenshots of texts she sent to Dickpimple's father telling on dipfuck and his bad behavior. Which brought daddy running to try and keep Dickpimple's shit straight. It was poetry in motion.

I tried to tell him that I can't feed one teenager on $200 per month much less two. His answer? "Once everything is finished with the divorce I'll see if I can help you." Me? Did you seriously just say, help ME? It's about our children ass-wipe, catch up.

> " *Jane2 was my Nuclear Option.* "

Which leads me to my next tip. DO NOT SEEK REVENGE. I didn't lash-out, I didn't smash his windshield or slash his expensive tires. I didn't post about it on social media ad nauseam, for real, don't do that. I didn't share intimate photos publicly to embarrass him. I didn't even slap him silly because, say it with me now – Prison orange is not my color, prison orange is not my color.

Don't add to your troubles by picking up criminal charges. The dick-weed isn't worth it.

Meanwhile, Dickpimple and Jane2 are sitting on $850,000 in assets on the two homes alone. I know because I searched them both up on county assessors' websites. Theirs is not going to be a quick divorce. You can clearly see Dickpimple left me no choice. I had to file for 100% custody plus the full amount of child support I should be getting to care for our children.

He vows to not pay me a penny and fight to keep 50% physical custody of them. So - let's see how that worked out for him. I share this sorry state of affairs with our mutual housekeeper, Jasmine PumperPatty. She immediately begins telling me exactly where the three-and-a-half-foot tall bong sits in the bathroom. On his toilet tank. So gross. How the stench of weed is so strong she doesn't know how he remains upright. Then she tells me my ex, and Jane2's soon-to-be ex, has acquired a roommate.

Another 50-something year old man, named Chip Knob Gobbler, who is also gainfully employed but for some reason has moved into the lake house with Dickpimple. The scene that keeps running through my head is Bert and Ernie doing their "roommates in the same bedroom" thing on Sesame Street. Around 2018, a former Sesame Street writer outed Bert and Ernie saying

> ❝ *Only the divorce attorneys win.* ❞

they are, as many of us have guessed and conjectured over the years, in fact gay. And Sesame Street execs reacted by trying to quiet the clamor by saying Bert and Ernie do not have a sexual orientation. Ouch, Sesame Street! Did you just gender neuter those Muppets? Not nice.

Both Jane and the housekeeper have wondered whether

Dickpimple and his friend are actually sharing the same Rubber Ducky at bath time. None of my business, but it's just gross.

Also none of my business but damn entertaining, Jane2 told me of Dickpimple's love of Botox. And I don't know what back alley he goes to for his wrinkle fighting injections, but she said one time it went terribly wrong and he couldn't open his eyes for a few days unless

> *We are all losers because we decided to get married.*

he pried them open with his fingers. Karma is a bitch, and she will show up on your doorstep. That's Karma at work right there, he always did lack vision. Jane2 said she laughed so hard and never let him live it down. And that's when she was still in love. Go, Jane2!

For my pending legal battle against Dickpimple, I'm gathering all the incoming intelligence, determining with my attorney which bits are in the children's best interest and served by me having 100% physical custody of them. I kept it all organized by category; texts, emails, lists of potential witnesses in case the courtroom could not be avoided. That witness list had Jane2's name at the very top and in red I wrote right next to it "Nuclear option". Always create your Nuclear Options checklist. Keep this a secret until the last minute. You don't want the enemy to find out about this.

The child support amount was a slam dunk, that's just an exercise in running the numbers through a set calculation. Oh, another one of Jane2's awesome assists to me was the information about which paperwork should be subpoenaed and where to look to capture his large, annual, bonuses, the only large thing about him., on top of his six-figure salary. I love that woman.

The motion to modify child support and custody was crafted and completed. After it was filed with the court, it was time for Dickpimple to find out I'm no longer fucking about, I'm coming for him... Actually just his cash.

It was on a sunny Saturday afternoon, just after he was served, I received a highly entertaining call from the divorce attorney's paralegal. My legal counsel hired the process server to hand deliver the court papers to Dickpimple. As the story goes the process server pulls up and she can't get in the gates of the exclusive golf club. So, she hoofs it up to his house where he's in the driveway.

> ❝ *We are going to have to hold an intervention the next time he announces marriage plans.* ❞

A guy with two women pissed off at him, both with legal standing, might feed some concern into a target when a woman walks up to him with what are clearly legal documents. The sperm-donor didn't have a clue. He graciously took the court papers, smiled, thanked the nice lady, and presumptuously said "This is from my current wife" and gives her a lift back to her car. The process server did tell the paralegal she wanted so much for dick-nozzle to read the documents while she was still in the car. To see his face the moment he realized it's actually his first ex-wife taking him to court to get his children and his money. He'll have to be patient while waiting to be served the divorce papers from Jane2.

> **As for me, I am done with both marriage and divorce.**

The sperm-donor and I went to mediation. Another life hack and pro tip for you is always mediate, if you can, don't litigate except as an absolute last-ditch effort. Mediate don't Litigate! You can imagine the satisfaction you would receive after a heart-pounding courtroom drama unfolds and climaxes as the judge proclaims you the rich victor and he, leaves in bloody rags. Umm, Yeah, no. It doesn't work that way.

As the saying goes, in that scenario only the divorce attorneys win.

Face it, we are all losers in this war because we were stupid enough to do one thing that doesn't work, we got married, followed by another colossal cluster fuck called divorce and that didn't work, either.

Don't waste a bunch of time and money on attorneys, spend it in therapy to get well and get through it, straighten your crown and get on with it. The day of mediation the mediator speaks to my attorney and me, first. Then he goes across the hall and speaks with Dickpimple and his attorney. Upon his return the mediator looks at me and, in all sincerity, and said "You are doing the exact right thing for your children. You're in the right." I'm no expert but I don't think mediators are meant to pick sides especially so early in the process, but it worked out so well! Not for Dickpimple, but for the kids and me.

All the things Dickpimple denied us for months were suddenly granted and the things he'd been demanding for months were taken from him. He lost custody of the kids and he can't get even partial custody back, or lower the child support amount, without sign off from a family counselor with a finding he and his home are fit for the kids. He'll never go to counseling which is why I can't believe he agreed to it!

You think I'm being harsh, don't you? But this case is mild compared to some. I should give the poor guy the benefit of the doubt, right? How could I possibly know he won't go to counseling?

Well, fun fact. When our marriage started going south like his limp Dickpimple we agreed to go to individual counseling with the goal of moving to couple's counseling and reconciliation. So that goes on for a couple of months and my counselor starts urging me to get Dickpimple on board for couple's counseling, it was time. Dickpimple wasn't having it, I kept covering for him by telling my psychologist he needed space and I didn't want to push or nag. Tip – don't waste your time and money on counseling

– one of you will bail or just not engage – and if you are lucky, one of you might change.

Then (you literally cannot make this shit up) I found out he never went to a counselor at all! Not once. He was boinking his girlfriend when he said he was going to counseling. Isn't that just a kick in the crotch fantastic?

> **" Don't waste your time or money on counseling, one of you just won't show yup. "**

Jane2 and I, Jane1, are going to have to hold an intervention the next time he announces marriage plans. We cannot responsibly sit idle by while he blows up some other fabulous woman's life. And there will be a third, fourth, fifth, etc, unless he is stopped. He's a serial marrier like his dad and my dad.

As for me I am Jane1 and DONE with both marriage and

divorce. They don't work.

I have my two amazing children, 100% custody and enough child support to properly care for them. I have a new friend and sisterhood with Jane2. We're like the "sister-ex-wives". That would make for a great reality show. In fact, speaking of therapy, free therapy, there are tons of groups, support groups that you need to join and hang out in. Not only does the free therapy work, but there is something to be said for hanging with the herd for protection. As for me, us ladies here in town created our own groups, because we

> **" Bed that HOT fuck-buddy. "**

didn't have any. So, now we have "The Hookers" (a.k.a. Los Hornitos) and "The Plastics" – which is actually a name taken from the movie Mean Girls, but so coined by one of my gay man friends. We need more "Damians" in this world.

The children only go to the lake house to see Bert and Ernie when they feel like it. And only for as long as they want to. The kids are so much more at peace. I encourage these visitations. The WASband is their sperm donor, after all, and I want him to have the opportunity to get it together and be in a good relationship with his wonderful kids. His behavior the last three decades indicates the chances of that happening are slim and none and Slim just walked out the door. Still, I like to think of myself as an optimist even where the fuck-nut mushroom-cap prune-pencil is concerned.

Never, ever, allow the sperm donor to forget this simple fact; the children did not ask to travel through his man tube to be brought into this family or this world.

The children have not committed the ridiculous act of getting married or divorced. That's all solely and squarely on both parents. Work it smarter, not harder, with all the tools at your disposal. Mediate rather than litigate.

You've got to remain alert. Just think if I'd not kept a

carefully pleasant relationship with Jane2 throughout her marriage to the douche-canoe, then befriend her in her time of tribulation. What if I'd not confided in the housekeeper, Jasmine Patty.

Lift each other up ladies, look for ways to support one another because you can tell a man exactly what you want but if you want it done right you just casually mention it in a conversation with a woman. Use your lady social skills.

The evening Jane2 told me "Thank you so much for confiding in her and explaining what happened to me. You've saved me months if not years of wondering what I did wrong, when I hadn't."

It wasn't you, Jane2. It wasn't me, Jane1. It was him, fucking Dickpimple.

Another proven pro tip, because I know ladies who've barreled back down the slippery slope. Under no circumstances make the same mistake twice. Do not marry a WASband, again. Sleep with him if you absolutely must. But under no circumstances should you enter into wedlock a second time to be reminded that marriage doesn't work and neither does divorce.

Ok, Lady's and Gent's ~ let's recap the strategic tips:

💔 Don't get married it doesn't work.

💔 Don't get divorced if you can avoid it, it doesn't work either.

💔 Don't make the same mistake twice.

💔 Don't take that raise or bonus, it will cause your alimony payments to go up.

💔 Hide your money – in cash.

💔 Change the locks, passwords on all your accounts, including the safe deposit box.

💔 Get a sentry biometric lock, you know the kind, don't give her the password.

💔 If you skeez, prevent da-sease.

💔 Use the legal system to bankrupt your ex.

💔 Attorneys and judges don't take an oath to tell the truth ~ use them to slander the bitch or asshole.

💔 Prepare for war ~ no matter how much you are both amicable in the beginning, it will turn nasty, don't give up anything and don't' promise anything, ever.

> *"Document Everything, Record Everything."*

💔 Tell the truth ~ of activities that prove you are a good person.

💔 Take pictures ~ with your kids.

💔 Document everything (Docs, Vids, Pics).

💔 Record everything.

💔 Don't leave the marital home, unless there's abuse and you have to get out!

💔 Anything and everything will be used in court, including text messages, voice calls, voice messages.

💔 Think with your brain, not your dick.

💔 Build a kick-ass legal team – read the reviews, and interview the lawyers to make sure they are going to kick-ass for you, and not get mowed over by the opposing counsel.

💔 Emptying the joint accounts – this could backfire on you when assets are divided by the court.

> " *Don't fuck your lawyer, ...or the judge.* "

💔 Talking trash – this makes you look like an ass, and it hurts the children. In some states its against the law.

💔 Posting on social media – turn off all social media accounts, make them private or delete them.

💔 Don't ever falsify anything – including accusations, documents, anything – be honest, upright and truthful, even when your partner isn't ~ the court will see it anyway.

💔 Don't start accumulating criminal charges ~ you can't even make harmless threats.

💔 Don't get angry.

💔 Do not harass or stalk your ex (see criminal charges above).

💔 No you can't take her wedding ring and hawk it ~ that's considered robbery (see criminal charges above).

💔 Join support groups ~ offline and online.

💔 Go to therapy.

💔 Change your will.

💔 Create a trust for you and your kids ~ without the ex of course.

💔 Don't fuck your lawyer.

💔 Don't fuck the judge.

💔 Don't take it out on the kids.

💔 You must be reasonable and calm – otherwise a judge will see you aren't and rule against you.

💔 Be respectful of everyone, including your ex.

💔 Dress well ~ first impressions never lie, especially in court.

💔 The Child support calculation is a formula also, and it can rarely be changed.

💔 Divorce diet ~ Remain HOT Always!

💔 NO divorce revenge ~ keep yourself OUT of jail, its no fun.

💔 Caveat to the "no divorce revenge" rule. The exception is getting your revenge by enjoying your new life out loud, and in full view, of the WASband whenever possible.

💔 Whatever happened to end the marriage, put it under the category of "None of my business". There is no point living in the past especially a heart-wrenching past.

💔 Head up, shoulders back, smile and laugh because the sooner you do, the longer you can make him absolutely miserable by proving you've moved on and you're better off without the cock-knocker wiggle~worm.

💔 Bed that young HOT fuck-buddy ~ and keep doing it.

💔 Come to peace with the fact marriage doesn't work and neither does divorce.

💔 It's important to remember if you see the opportunity, absolutely make the WASband's next divorce work for you.

💔 Befriend the second wife, get in tight with the mutual housekeeper, and any other "spys" or "moles" you can plant in the other organization (family) that will be loyal to you with critical intelligence.

💔 If you can't join 'em, build 'em. Support groups that is, and use your imagination...ya, ask Gay people to name your group. Keep your kids out of it ~ be the bigger person.

THE MODERN EVOLUTION...

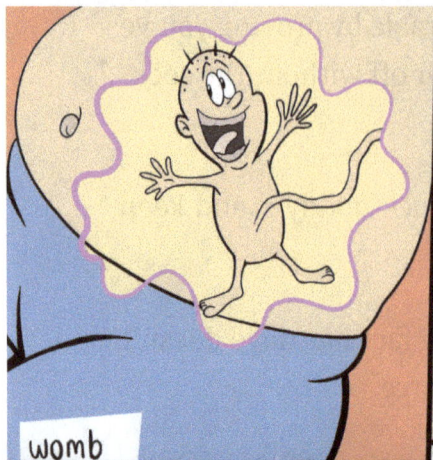

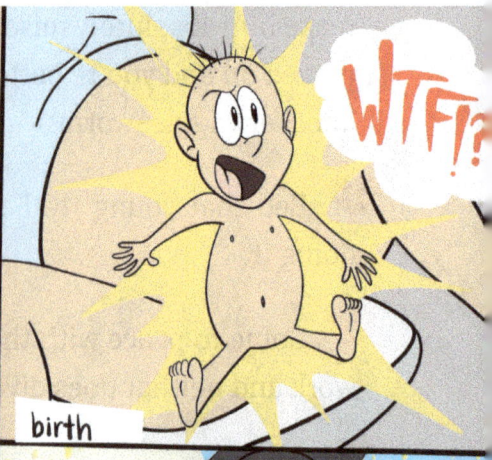

Marriage Doesn't Work

...AND DESCENT OF MAN

Neither Does Divorce

Marriage Doesn't Work

#GROWaPAIR
#WARNINGtrauma
#MENareVICTIMStoo
#exposeTHEnarc
#TRUEstory
#happened

Officer Friendly

"Divorce - Latin, Meaning to rip a man's genitals out through his wallet." (borrowed from Robin Williams, RIP)

~Rory SchwänzLecken, Random Ghost Author

◇◇

WARNING: Child Trauma, Abuse, Domestic Violence, Random Lies and Bullshit

◇◇

Sedona, Arizona...early 2000's. I was on a bit of a spiritual healing path at the time because I had just gotten sober in Reno, NV. I was looking for all forms of spiritual healing, so I popped into a psychic to see what would happen. She told me about the "Crossing of the Saints" at Santa Cruz, CA ... which was close to my home. She had a crystal ball, the flowing drapes, the incense... the whole 9 yards. The interesting part was when I was leaving... I randomly, intuitively asked her if there is a book I should read. Not really sure why that came out of my mouth. She glanced around the room, walked over to the corner and picked one up and handed it to me. As if, she just randomly picked one off the shelf. I didn't think anything of it. The book was the "Way of the Peaceful Warrior" by Dan Millman. I read it word for word, front to back, cover to cover. It was a little funky but it was magic. It spoke to me, I felt it.

> **" She had a crystal ball, flowing drapes, incense, the whole 9 yards. "**

As the psychic was previously telling me my "fortune",

she said I would meet the woman of my dreams, she would be sexy, intelligent, powerful and healthy. There wouldn't be any co-dependence or other non-grown-up traits about her. It would be the woman I would marry. She was right about the positive traits, but maybe she didn't have all of the information. Or maybe she flat out lied. I don't know.

1980's, somewhere in the clutches of Southern California, was a little girl growing up who randomly had an interaction with a psychic. That psychic gave the little girl a spoon, and at the top of that little spoon was a Masonic symbol. The little girl held onto that spoon her entire life.

> **" She said I would meet the woman of my dreams. "**

As the little girl grew into teen-hood, she eventually landed a scholarship at the University of California,

Berkeley. This young lady Majored in English Literature History. Her favorite book of all time turned out to be... "Way of the Peaceful Warrior" by Dan Millman. Coincidentally, the events that Dan Millman wrote about took place in Berkeley, CA.

2007. We met through a match making agency, a very personal one, not the online match dot bomb type of services. The iPhone and Tinder didn't even exist yet. The lady that was doing the matchmaking seemed to have come out of nowhere, and it was almost as if she was psychic. My bride and I dated a couple of times and then eloped to Las Vegas and got married. I was getting old and the pickin's was slim in San Jose, CA. She had what I wanted. Sexy, employed (so I was led to believe), wanted to get married, had not been married before and she wanted kids. It was perfect. We were infatuated with each other. The sex was hot and heavy, and often. She was a little top heavy, but I liked that.

Right after we returned from Vegas, we moved all of

her stuff into my place. As we were packing, her kitchen stuff I noticed in amongst the silverware drawer, hidden underneath all the other silverware that actually gets used, was this cute little teaspoon, with a Masonic emblem at the top of it. Hmm, I thought that was strange, so I said to my new bride, "you know I'm a California Mason right?" She didn't know, grabbed the spoon and put it in the packing box. After that, I learned that my new bride would go on to keep this little treasure in her jewelry box as if it had some magical power. She said a psychic gave it to her, whom also told her that she would marry a Masonic man someday. She still has it, to this day, even though we are now divorced, and she has re-married. That's where the dream ends and the horror begins.

After the Vegas nuptials, I had a taste of her cooking. Well, actually she didn't know how to cook, so I made spaghetti... easy enough. We got into an argument over who should be driving my brand new Mercedes Benz. When I told her no, she threw a plate of spaghetti in my face, plate and all. That should have been the first red flag.

> **"She asked if I would be interested in attending therapy."**

I should have annulled the marriage and moved on. But, I was raised in a "Religious" family and you were supposed to "stick it out", and "make it work". Divorce was a sin. So, I stayed.

A couple of months into this marriage and my bride was asking if I would like to attend Marriage Counseling. Um, I found that to be really odd, especially so early in the relationship. That should have been another red flag. So, we started going to our first therapy sessions. After a couple of "both partners together" sessions, with both of us in the room, she flaked out and never went again. I assumed it was my responsibility to keep going, so I did.

Shortly after moving all of her stuff in to my condo, she proceeded to tell me that she wasn't actually working, but out on disability, claiming a back injury or some bullshit like that. Apparently she had been working for a Police Department in Northern

> ## " *That was the first red flag.* "

California for the past five years, and was BS'ing the injury so she could collect on her pension for the rest of her life... like one of her close friends did previously. Apparently this game is common. She was really healthy, I'll give her that, she used to run all the time and competed in Triathlon's, Sprint's and Olympic's. At least until the insurance company showed up to one of the races and took pictures of her running, obviously without any back pain. She was charged with workers compensation fraud and had to settle out of court, forfeiting her pension.

It gets worse.

My Bride suffered from depression. I had the same affliction but had been managing it successfully for years before we met. She had suicidal ideation (thoughts), would tell me she hated her life and wanted to die. This was a continual event throughout our marriage. It got so bad, that less than a year after we were married she admitted herself to a psych hospital. The Doctor diagnosed her with Dissociative Identity Disorder (DiD), the new name for Borderline Personality Disorder (BPD). In hindsight, this would explain a ton of shit later.

She tried medication but hated it and never tried it again. The multiple personalities were definitely showing up now. It wasn't until after this, that I had found out she had been abused as a child, sexually, physically and verbally.

> *I was now getting to see her true colors.*

She was raped in front of her mother, by her Uncle. One reason why she hates her family. My heart sunk. I didn't know what to do. I loved her and I wanted the best for her. But I was now getting to see Her Majesties Royal Highness Femme Officer

Friendly's true colors. While turbulent, her up-bringing was under the auspices of a trust fund daddy, so she carried this sense of entitlement everywhere, combined with an over-bearing, no, over-demanding, ball busting narcissistic rage.

> *Her lover's shirt said "my dick fell off".*

Financial Abuse.

When we were dating I asked her how her credit was. She said it was "Great". I later found out that she had bad credit, a spending problem and had kept refinancing her condo to pay off cards, and then charge them back up again. The Loan to Value ratio was so high on her Condo that when the real estate market crashed, she had to file bankruptcy. And yes, she could have gotten a job to make the payments, but she did not like that idea for some reason. Because she was married now (to me), she honestly figured she didn't need to work. Remember the entitlement piece to her personality... That carried on even after divorce.

Not too long after that, Officer Friendly took a trip to Cabo San Lucas with one of her friends, who turned out to be her lesbian lover ... I later discovered. I should have known something was up, her lover would pick her up and ride off on her Harley. She had tats and piercings, which I don't object to. Her lover used to wear a shirt that said "My dick fell off". Their excuse was they were going to AA meetings. Later found out those were LGBT AA meetings. It's rather ironic, as officer friendly would often accuse me of being Gay. While vacationing in Cabo, she and her lover bought a timeshare under both of their names. She kept

> **_She went on a shopping spree, not buying Christmas presents for anyone else._**

this hidden from me for years before she admitted it to me. For those of you new at this, when you get married, any financial transaction you make while married affects both of you. Reason number 2053 not to get married.

At one point I gave her my credit card to do some Christmas Shopping, and she went on a shopping spree for herself. I still had to buy presents for the other people. She felt she "deserved" it. I know this is trivial; however, it shows the gross negligence that a marriage contract imposes on people's financial well being.

> *"She never cooked. She didn't know how to."*

I would give her money to buy food for the entire household, and she would never buy food for me. When I asked what am I supposed to do for food, her response was consistently, "Starve". She never cooked... ever. She

> **"** 3 in 10 women, 1 in 10 men that have experienced rape, physical & mental violence, abuse, or stalking by a partner, report that it has had an impact on their functioning **"**

~ *Random Fact*

didn't know how to. I had to make my own meals. Which, in today's society where roles have changed, that should almost be expected. I mean, I keep hearing more and more about how Men do the cooking and cleaning. I'm fine with it.

I supported her through Law School. All good. She didn't work the entire time. In fact, she never worked when we were married, even though she was fully capable of it. After three years of Law School, co-signing her student loans and three bar exam attempts at $2k a pop, she just one day said "I don't want to be a lawyer". I was beyond pissed. At this point, I was just numb and getting used to the abuse.

> **"** *I hit the pavement face first, and she just left me there.* **"**

I found myself financing her mani/pedi's, salon visits,

gym memberships, chiropractor visits, etc... I loved her, and enjoyed doing this for her... at least for a little while. Slowly I would get a resentment here and there. I was always super laid back so the narcissistic control creeping in didn't phase me, or I didn't really notice. My family noticed, but they continued to support us.

> **" She was ready to let me die right there, on the side of the road. "**

Physical Abuse.

After our first child was born, we moved to a different state where they had better schools, and a better quality of life for our kid. My bride didn't give a shit, she was glad she was going to get to travel to a new state. When we got there we would have one more kid. We now have two boys whom I love and adore and doing everything for.

I remember the stress of being around my bride was so bad at times, I would end up in the hospital or urgent care for "GI Issues" of unknown origin. The Doctor's just sent me home after running tests. Inconclusive. One time in 2011, I had some really bad lung infection, I pulled over to let her drive. I opened the door and fell out onto the pavement face first. My lovely bride just left me there. She called 911. My one year old was in his car seat in the back. When I awoke, there were two strangers hovering over me, and yelling back to my bride, "He's awake"... She was busy flirting with the officer talking about when the

> **She is stunningly beautiful, and that is deceiving.**

"bus" (ambulance) would arrive. I recovered, and left the emergency room with a few stitches to my face. All tests ... inconclusive. That was the day I realized I wasn't in a loving relationship, and it probably wouldn't last if I was concerned for my own well being. She clearly didn't give a shit about me. She was ready to let me die right there on the side of the road.

As time progressed in the marriage, we would start in with new therapists. And then her habit of attending twice and never again was almost predictable. A couple of therapists she flat out fired, because they weren't doing what she wanted.

Our dearest Officer Friendly is stunningly beautiful. But outward appearances are deceiving. Inside the household, she is very demanding and mean. Our relationship was very similar to the situation portrayed in the movie "Sleeping With The Enemy" yet with roles reversed.

Her demand for perfection reached unrealistic bounds, for example she would yell at me if the towels weren't folded "correctly". The towels were never folded "correctly". On two occasions, My Bride had gone into the closet, taken all of my clothes and thrown them on the ground, demanding that I fold them the "right" way – while

> **" The books had to be lined up perfectly. "**

her clothes remain in a pile and disorganized on her side of the closet. The children's books had to be put back in the bookshelf ... "perfectly"... Tallest on the left, gradually the next tallest, and so on, so the book on the far right was the shortest. The spine of the book had to be about a half an inch from

> **" Her demand for perfection reached unrealistic bounds. "**

the edge, all of them. It was so razor sharp, it seemed impossible and scary. It was real yet bizarre... surreal. My mother was visiting once, after reading to my kid, she put the books on the top of the bookshelf and soon received the wrath of her majesty. The control gradually got worse.

> **" I have been punched, slapped, kicked, heeled and bullied. "**

There were times when I was not allowed to use the kitchen or bathrooms – and I still don't know why. The doors to all the rooms in the house had to be shut and closed, and when they weren't there was hell to pay.

Everyday it seems like, My Bride would get upset at me for "not doing something right" and would sometimes hit me. I have been punched, slapped, kicked, heeled and bullied by Officer Friendly over the course of our marriage.

My bride said she likes rough sex. I don't share that desire.

One time during sex she slapped me so hard in the face, two times, that my ears started ringing and have been ringing ever since then. I think that is what triggered my tinnitus, but everyone in my age group has it, so whatever... I'm shopping around for hearing aides now. Her thing was to have a porn movie going, black-guy on white-girl, and then start riding me, to get herself off, she would start slapping me violently saying "You like watching that porn?" "Do Ya?" I really didn't, but whatever she wanted, she got. She had this vibrator 'kit', a big machine thing with inter-changeable penis covers. Because I wasn't big enough, She made me wear one of the inter-changeable penises. Worked nicely actually, as I didn't have to wear a condom. When we went to have kids, she would just bend over and say "Hurry up monkey, I don't really like having you on my back".

> **Men don't bruise like women do.**

During sex, I have been slapped in the face so many times, and I think the tinnitus condition is getting worse. I hear ringing in my ears, and when telling my former bride of this, her response is "yeah right, get over it". Always, like a true narcissist, total denial of any part in the wrongdoing. Blind or ignorant, you pick.

> **"Why would I file a police report, she was the police."**

Her favorite line, which is actually kind of funny was "Grow a pair!".

Being around my bride had my stress level very high, because I was always in fear of what she will do to me next. It started to happen every day. Sometimes it would subside, but would always return to the yelling. You know like a roller coaster, up and down, but always growing over time.

As time went on, I found my health declining, because I wasn't allowed to take care of myself, I was so focused on her wants and needs. I started jogging with her while she ran, so I could get some exercise. Not a good idea starting up a running career in your mid 40's never having done it before. I tore my ACL and had to have knee surgery. The very next day while recovering, one of her dogs got loose, and she made me chase it down, in pain and all. I'm sure that is why my knee has never fully recovered. The physical therapist said that surgery now would just make it worse.

> **" The abuse slowly escalated. "**

My rotator cuff's are torn on both shoulders, but was really bad on the right side. Stress had me in the hospital again, and when they were trying to figure everything out, they noticed another kidney stone developing in my right side. My bride shortly after that said "You can't have any more surgeries, tough it out." I wasn't allowed to see Doctor's or have surgeries any more, yet my Bride was continuing with her Doctor, Chiropractor and Massage appointments. She had hip surgery once, and blamed it on the law enforcement agency she was working at in Colorado. When, in reality she fucked her body up from all that running and races.

The physical abuse slowly escalated.

One day Officer Friendly found a receipt from Chipotle that I took our son to for Lunch. She cornered me when I was sitting on the toilet (A common narcissist attack method) and beat the shit out of me. She acted like I had committed murder or cheated or something. Over a diet coke. Did I mention she was

> "*I had to use the porta-pottie across the street in the park.*"

controlling my diet? I wasn't allowed to drink Diet Coke or eat sweets at all. I wasn't and still am not diabetic either.

I've had my head beat for eating her Almonds. I've been beat up and punched in a fit of rage for eating her pineapple. Again, I asked what to do for food, and she said

"YOU HAVE TO STARVE!".

Officer Friendly did not do relationships very well in any area of her life. She never could get along with my parents who were the sweetest people in the world. She had cut off communication completely with her Mom, Dad and Brother, for reasons I'm not sure of. One time she started a fight with my parents in a restaurant, right after our second child was born. My parents had to leave and stay in a hotel, putting my mother in tears, never to return to our household again.

> **" *Putting a one-litre Pepsi bottle up to my ass wasn't going to work very well.* "**

The control was becoming unlivable. For a period of time, I wasn't allowed to use any of the bathrooms or toilets in the house. That was fine when I could do my conference calls from coffee shops. When I returned home, she screamed at me to use the outhouse, porta-potties across the street at the park. I did. Even if it was in the middle of the winter and freezing outside. I had setup my "office" in the unfinished basement of our home, and had to pee in a large empty, one-liter Pepsi bottle so I could remain on the conference calls without leaving the house. One day I was having bowel problems, and had to put the people on hold and run across to the porta-pottie four times to take a shit. I mean putting a one-litre Pepsi bottle up to my ass wasn't going to work very well

> **"The abuse began to nip at my Son, and that is where it got to be too much."**

in my mind. I just didn't want to do the cleanup. That was fucking exhausting. The resentments grew strong that day. One time, my son and I were playing with Lego's in the basement, and we both ran upstairs to pee really fast. Officer Friendly had a sixth sense. She knew what we had done immediately and came down to the basement in a rage, screaming and yelling "I TOLD YOU MOTHERFUCKERS NOT TO USE THE BATHROOM!".

The abuse began to nip at my son. And this is where it got to be too much.

Mental Abuse.

Her Majesty controlled my every movement. I wasn't allowed to do anything unless she approved. I was

> **"A complete conversation took multiple phone calls."**

surprised I was still employed. Seriously, my employer put up with a ton of shit from me because I was constantly tending to her needs and wants. I was forbidden from communicating with my family, my parents and siblings without first asking her. Whenever I would send emails to my parents, I had to CC her.

Mer Majesty was not only physically abusive, but verbally and mentally abusive as well. She had an anger problem what would show up daily. It was never a loving and intimate tone, but rather a deleterious and demanding bark that would escalate into physical violence. She went to an anger management class early in our marriage, but she quit after the first session.

Her Majesty RoboBop always had house rules. She needed to feel in control of everything, all of the time. I understand some of them, but they were ridiculous. The infamous one was we were never allowed to fart or burp ... inside the house. It was verboten. This really sucked because my boys and I love the sound of farts. We even have a fart gun and it's a fucking riot.

Officer Friendly never had a complete conversation with me on the phone. She would call, escalate into a rage and then hang up on me. If she had more than one sentence to say, she would call multiple times, rage and hang up. This went on for years and years. A complete conversation would take several phone calls. It's sounds funny in retrospect, but was very painful and would get my nerves on edge. It would literally take hours for me to get over one of those calls.

There were never "Asks", but always "Demands" and "Orders". I did everything in that household, yes, everything, with no help from anyone else in that house.

In one of her disassociative fugue's I returned home from taking our son to school, and she started yelling at me angrily for putting

> *" Why are you so fucking stupid? "*

my clothes on the bed, saying "why are you so fucking stupid?" over and over again. Then she wailed on me 4-5 times while I was holding our newborn baby. She followed up by saying "I FUCKING HATE YOU, YOU PIECE OF SHIT" several times. This happened so often, I was sort of used to the trauma, and was numb to it. I couldn't see a path free if it hit me in the face.

She had a habit of calling me "FUCKING STUPID" so many times during our marriage, that I soon started to believe she was right. To this day, I question my smarts and intelligence, or maybe the lack thereof. I used to be strong and confident before we met, but I have withered into a small, lost, soul-less, spineless papier-mâché Mannequin. I know this is affecting my kids. "I need to protect them" started flowing through my head.

> **" *I know this is affecting my kids, I need to protect them.* "**

In another fugue, her Royal Highness grabbed a golf

club and ran around the house pummeling the custom granite, stone work and woodwork throughout the house. Smartphones are handy when you need to record this type of activity. I submitted this to my lawyer, and they still wouldn't give me an RO - Restraining Order. When people came over to visit, we had to put vases and flower pots in front of the damage to cover it up.

> **" I fucking hate kids, get away from me! "**

That night I had a dream that I was at the driving range hitting the sweet spot on every ball in an endless supply just rolling onto the carpet for me to energize. I looked up and there she was, covering her face, in the kitchen. Unfortunately my swing ain't that good, and balls were hitting everything except her, glass was breaking, neighbors were in the streets gawking. Then I heard my kid, "Daddy?", I woke up to his beautiful face standing next to my bed. It was surreal.

The flowers, I have to mention the flowers, because it's fucking hilarious. I didn't mind buying flowers for my bride. But she demanded it, weekly. I always went out of my way during my work day, to get "over the top flowers" for her. Two dozen roses, lilys and stuff, and when I brought them home, she would always make me take them back because they were "too ugly". This happened weekly.

> ## " *When mommy yells at me, it takes all of the greatness out of me.* "

At one point, she was so angry at the flower situation that she mentioned that she wanted to "eat her gun". One time, I had to return to the store 18 times before I finally ended with an assortment that pleased her. The guy at the store was gay, and felt sorry for me, so every time I came in, he took the matter into his own hands, and made sure it was an over the top bouquet. I never said anything and when he saw me returning, he just went to work again and handed me another over the top bouquet. Got to be good friends with that guy.

On one Tuesday, it had snowed that day. It was a snow day, and Officer Friendly had the day off. The house was starting to get a little disorganized, meaning the beds weren't made, the daily dog hair wasn't vacuumed from the floor, ... it was still clean but it wasn't razor sharp spotless in other words. She freaked out, started yelling at the kids, saying "I FUCKING HATE KIDS, GET AWAY FROM ME" to the children. She often yells at my son and it makes him break out in tears. I cry every time I think about the damage that is being done to him.

> *She yelled, I FUCKING HATE YOU! nose-to-nose, to my kid's face.*

One night while my son was helping me do the dishes, my bride was sitting in bed playing with her iPhone. My son imparted to me, "I don't like getting yelled at." I responded "I know honey, you know I think you are great and amazing". Then he said, "When mommy yells at me, it takes all of the greatness out of me, and I don't feel great anymore".

> **"I knew an immense amount of damage had already been done."**

My heart sank. Not just sank. I felt an uneasy imblance in my chest, as if I swallowed some noxious liquid and it was burning me up from the inside out. My arms grew weak. My spine and legs tingled. The hair on my head and arms got a boner as the noxious ball of hurt slowly travelled down my body to my feet. Hurt, pain, sadness, disbelief, shock and you know that feeling of being imobilized by fear... all hit me at once. Maybe I really was fucking stupid, because I didn't know what to do, or where to go. I cried for my boy.

One evening, I was in Washington, DC on business. My son called me using mommy's phone, crying, balling his eyes out because mommy called him "a dummy". She said she apologized, and was having a bad day, and that he wasn't listening. Officer Friendly had a bad day everyday.

> **"Mommy said she was going to kill me."**

One time, after spending the whole day with our oldest son, she was frustrated, and I can understand that. But what came next at the end of the day was unacceptable. My son and I were in the hallway by his bedroom. Officer Friendly was having another bad day. She was in her closet for some reason, and she just randomly started screaming, "I'VE HAD ENOUGH OF YOUR SHIT!" She came running out of the closet, full bore, pedal down, balls-out, ripping down the hallway and straight up to my kid's face as he was cowering in the corner, and said "I FUCKING HATE YOU" hunched over, right into his face, nose to nose, at the top of her lungs. My son was devastated and started crying. All I could do was try to hold and coddle him, but I knew an immense amount of damage had already been done. That was the last straw for me. At that point I was done.

> **" *Judges and lawyers don't take an oath, only you do.* "**

Kids mis-behave and that sometimes pushes parents to the edge. But there is the edge, and then there is over the edge. Our oldest son (5 at the time) had been misbehaving badly, throwing tantrums, getting angry and throwing things. I think he learned this from watching Officer Friendly in action. He would take toys away from his baby brother. One time he hid Officer Friendly's crutches so she wouldn't be able to walk after hip surgery. Ok, that was funny actually. However, the bride has a short fuse, she snapped and told my son she was going to "KILL HIM". My kid came running to me saying that "Mommy said she was going to kill me".

Another time our oldest son broke out in tears as he witnessed Officer Friendly flip into a rage and come at me with a knife in her hand saying "I'M GOING TO FUCKING KILL YOU"... not in a joking way, but in an, oh shit she is about to kill me... kinda way. My boy cried in my arms for hours after that.

> **" Divorce is harder than death. "**

I don't know why I stayed over the years. There is a lot more to this story, but I need to save some space, and not ramble on. There was so much more abuse. Much more trauma. But when it started to affect my children in large part, is when I started shopping for a legal team. A fucked up marriage, and now a fucked up divorce – the two most painful experiences a person can have in life. These experiences will literally kill you, destroy your soul, take everything you have and leave you penniless and destitute.

July 24, 2017 ~ I finally "grew a pair" and left the marriage. I moved out. Got an apartment and started rebuilding.

> *" I want my alimony payment, as she stood there wrapping her lips in lipstick. "*

Lawyers will tell you to "Stay in the marital home". Bullshit, get out and save your ass while you can. That house will be sold anyway. Don't ever let a lawyer tell you what to do if your life or your children's lives are in danger. The Lawyers just want to you keep the house so they can suck the equity out of it to pay their fees.

Her sixth sense kicked in. When I was signing my lease, she was calling and texting me incessantly. She knew. She was going to lose control of me, and that was terrifying to her.

I am a great provider, I work hard. I pay for everything and I do all of the work around the house. Gender roles have changed. What was good for your parents, ain't gonna work this time for you. Just know that up front.

411 ~ all of the dirt will come out in the Divorce, so get ready for an ass lashing. But make sure you document everything, record everything (audio and video) and take pictures.

If you think Marriage is hard, some people compare Divorce as "harder than death". It's actually pretty damn true. It's a fucking horror in all the worst ways possible. Just when you think it can't get any worse, lawyers step in to use their dirty tricks and you will find yourself saying "No fucking way" opposing counsel is doing this right now. Yep, they uncover evil shit, I mean evil shit that will fuck with you and your children. Lawyers make shit up that never happened. It doesn't matter that you are the awesome parent of the century. You will be painted as the worst parent ever. Trust me, if they can't find any dirt on you, they will flat out lie and make shit up. And it's legal. Judges and Lawyers don't take an oath to tell the truth and nothing but the truth... only you do.

The day after I left, I went to the marital home, and my ex-bride was actually somewhat lucid and calm. She agreed to a divorce, and we filed papers amicably. I understand there are formulas for alimony and child support, and these can easily be calculated at https://www.familylawsoftware.com/.[6] Btw: It's never amicable.

The next day when we met with the Family Court Facilitator, Officer Friendly mentioned how she deserved the $4500 a month alimony and child support because she had worked for it. There's that sense of entitlement again. She felt she "deserved" it. For someone who was always toting the fact that she was a hard core Republican, she was always acting like a Democrat, expecting handouts because she "deserved" it. The FCF looked at her with the face of "WTF?".

Shortly after this I figured my ex bride was pissed about me leaving, because as I was pulling up to a restaurant to grab some grub, the back window of my SUV suddenly shattered. I never did find the spent bullets.

Unknown to me prior to this event, my ex-bride – whom I walked out on – had already begun scouting. She was doing this long before I left. She probably sensed it coming. She had her barrel sighted on her next victim. Our Divorce decree was final Feb 2018. Exactly one month later, Officer Friendly became someone else's new bride. She remarried. I filed a motion to terminate alimony. Because, as we all know, when you re-marry, you forfeit the right to alimony from your previous spouse that was paying you because you now have new financial support. This enraged my former bride, even though she was still receiving child support to the tune of $1k a month. The alimony was around $3500 a month, give or take. Some couples get less, some get more ... it's all based on the calculation, and you can't really mess with the algorithm. If you do, or someone does, then you've been given a bad

hand. And believe me some judges will alter this formula just to make you pay. Gender doesn't matter really, I've

Marriage Doesn't Work

seen some male judges hand ex-husband's some pretty fucked up deals... even though the calculation formula says what it says. This is why I think the Divorce Empire and the players in it, are corrupt.

When you are embroiled in a Divorce, what you think is fair ... isn't. What you think is reasonable ... isn't. It's all what the lawyers jockey for, and what the judge ends up thinking is fair based on the information provided by the lawyers. Even the Court Family Investigators (CFI) and Parent Responsibilities Evaluators (PRE) are corrupt and have jaded opinions. If you are male, and the CFI or PRE hates men, your fucked. If you are female, and the CFI or PRE hates women, you're fucked too. Even then judges do some off the wall shit, you be thinking like, "what is she on" I wonder... Lawyers are master's at lying and they will. In fact, judges and lawyers don't have to take an oath to "tell the truth and nothing but the truth"... before they start looking over your data. They can do whatever the fuck they want, make up any facts they want, and you are stuck with the consequences for the rest of your life. And all of these corrupt a-holes sit there and say "it's all about the children now". They could care the fuck less about your children, it's a straight up money game to them. Ain't that a final bitch blow.

We are still in a nasty custody battle because she is still pissed of she didn't get her chunk of Alimony for the rest of her life. And, well, the lawyers and judges need to feed their family too. She is jockeying for more parenting time, to turn that $1000 child support into $2000 a month. The total cost of this escapade will be around $50,000 each, maybe more and for how much will she gain? Make sure you do the math on the whole project people. $100,000 to get an extra $1000. It will take 10 years to make that money back. It has nothing to do with spending more time with the kids, she just wants more money. And quite frankly the kids want nothing to do with her and they cry every time they have to go over to mommas house. My ten year old has it figured out now, but my six year old runs and hides under his bed every time his mom comes to pick him up. It's heartbreaking because I know what he is running from...and it's terror.

To pour gasoline on the fire, her royal highness decided it would be a good idea to have one of the teachers at our kids school file a false DHS report - Department of Human Services. Here where I live that is equivalent to Child Protective Services. A few months later, she herself, filed a false DHS report. Did I have a right to see the reports ... absofuckinglutely. And I did. The first report was total BS, saying my kids were in danger when living with me because my oldest only had a piece of bacon for breakfast. The second report said the kids were in danger when living with me because they don't bathe, go barefoot in the house, don't brush their teeth, and aren't fed "properly". More BS. The only truth in that is of course my kids take off their shoes when they enter my home, I like to keep it clean. Thankfully, DHS ruled that there was nothing of concern and closed the files. But this is the kind of bullshit that is waged against fathers, just so the mother can get more money. It isn't right, but it's not illegal either.

After all of these years. I love my boys, give them hugs, tell them I love them, and give them kisses and they reply in kind. When they are with me, we facetime Grandma and Grandpa, Aunts and Uncles, Cousins and their Babies, because they are the only family they have ever known. The Ex is a master at Familial Alienation, but now that I have escaped I plan to keep my boys close to my family. The boys have never met the other side of the family, but I'm friends with them on social media, so I introduce them to their family through pictures. If the ex found out, she would go nuclear. My boy's know whats up, and I intend to give them the best life I possibly can... without including her, well because that would be counter to a good life. Interestingly enough, not once, in the past 14 years, did Her Majesties Royal Highness Femme Officer Friendly ever say "I love you", nor "I'm sorry". That just wasn't in her vocabulary I guess.

~~~ WHAT TO EXPECT ~~~

~~~ BEFORE ~~~

~~~ AFTER ~~~

Man Cave Rules:

My boys and I came up with Man Cave rules for Daddy's new apartment. There are many examples of these "Man Cave Rules" around, but we made our own... and these rules are legit 'cause they weren't allowed in the house of pain.

- Pee like a man ~ standing up.

- Leave the toilet seat up.

- Fart early, Fart often.

- Belch whenever you want.

- Eat whatever the fuck you want, whenever you want.

- It's ok to scratch, snort and spit.

💀 No whining, bitching or moaning.

💀 Grow a pair.

💀 Screen time and video games are always allowed.

💀 Speak freely, using any form of language and words you prefer (swearing included, after all this isn't a fucking church guys).

💀 Men have feelings, and we talk about them here. Yes, that's right, read it again.

💀 Don't be a dick.

💀 Seriously don't be a dick.

Marriage Doesn't Work

My Good~Dad Deeds List:

There are a lot of good Dads out there. Roles have changed, and the Men are stepping up but not getting recognized for their efforts. Here is my list of things that Good Dads do, I'm sure you can add to it.

🔶 I was continuously employed, and a great provider.

🔶 I did all of the dish washing, drying and putting away.

🔶 I washed the laundry, dried it, folded it and put it away.

🔶 I vacuumed the entire house at least once a day. The carpet had to have "rows" in it like a model home. If it wasn't done right, I had to do it again.

🔶 I took out the garbage.

SUPER DAD I washed out, bleached and sanitized the garage once a week … we had a dog, but she was forced to live in the garage … even during winter. That poor thing. She died a few years later.

SUPER DAD I did everything for the kids. Fed them, gave them baths, woke them up, got them ready for school, brushed their teeth, packed their lunches, took them to school, picked them up from school, took them to sports activities.

SUPER DAD I was always buying new clothes, shoes and winter gear for the kids.

SUPER DAD I was always taking the boys to get their haircuts.

SUPER DAD We would eat out a lot because the bride didn't cook.

I taught the kids...

SUPER DAD How to ride bikes.

SUPER DAD How to write computer code.

SUPER DAD How to create their own social media video channel.

SUPER DAD How to swim.

SUPER DAD How to tie their shoes.

SUPER DAD How to dress themselves and put dirty clothes in the hamper.

SUPER DAD How to build Legos and Lego Trains.

SUPER DAD How to build Hotwheels tracks.

SUPER DAD How to build Lincoln Logs.

SUPER DAD How to build solar powered robots.

SUPER DAD I have been totally involved in our Kids

school activities, volunteering, starting an after-school coding club, and chaperoning on field trips.

I read them books before bed, and they are starting to read to me. I would take the boys to the library to pick out books to read at home.

I taught them how to deal with mean people and bully's at school.

I take the boys everywhere with me.

To the park to ride their bikes and scooters.

I take them to soccer practice and games.

I take them to their swimming lessons.

I take them to their birthday parties.

I take them to their karate lessons.

I take them to lacrosse practice and games.

SUPER DAD I take them to Boy Scouts until that organization folded.

SUPER DAD I take them to the Doctor when they get sick.

SUPER DAD I take them to the hospital for emergencies.

SUPER DAD I take them to their eye doctors. My son would pick out a pair of glasses he liked, and the ex would tell him "NO", and force him to wear glasses that she picked out. I would spend $700 on a pair of glasses for my kid and she would trash them, and force me to pay half of the pair she wanted.

Marriage Doesn't Work

Solutions

CoHabi~Couples

"Love is blind, it's time to open your eyes, before the real damage is done."

~Ricard SchlaffSchaft, Random Ghost Author

I obviously don't have all of the answers. And I'm certainly no expert. However I am educated. I do have a lot of experiences, and I have common-sense.

It would seem reasonable to me that as a society we should make Marriage illegal, or remove it from it's legality. Divorce as a concept should be non-existent at that point.

Ban marriage and ban divorce.

Make "Partnering" for the sole sake of reproduction a thing. If you must, get everything in writing up front, including dissolution and separation and the terms of it. - in a partnership agreement. And if there isn't one, there should be one applied by default. By default, without an agreement it should be 50/50 for all assets obtained during the partnership, and 50/50 parenting.

That means 50/50 everything for the kids. You can argue that so-and-so makes more money, and kids are expensive, but honestly, basic necessities aren't expensive, you each can handle 50/50.

Alimony is pure bullshit anyway, so there will be no such thing moving forward. Everyone is now equal, everyone works for a living and can support themselves, there is no need to keep on taxing a partner that you have

> **" *Marriage and Divorce should be removed from society.* "**

made a decision to leave. It doesn't matter if one partner leaves, and the other partner still wants the partnership - the partnership has dissolved and you both should go your different ways, supporting yourselves independently.

> ## *"50/50 for the kids, and 50/50 for acquired assets, thats it, nothing more!"*

The partnership separation process should only be allowed to use a filing system with the county recorder to make it official. No judges, no lawyers, no exorbitant fees for a bunch of bullshit and lies.

Before you partner-up, declare a simple agreement. Anything acquired during the partnership gets split. Most likely you will choose 50/50.

No alimony. It's bullshit anyway.

If you have children you will support them according

> ## *No Alimony, No more Child Tax.*

to your agreement. By default it will be 50/50. And all expenses should be tracked and reconciled electronically so there is no overpayment, or abuse of funds. Ex: Kids need food, buy the food, submit the receipt, and get reimbursed for half. Thats it. Sorry, if you submit a receipt for a salon or vacation, that won't be reimbursable. Corporations have this accountability, so should people in relationships.

No more bullshit formulas because that person makes more money, etc.

It's simple, it's clean, it's efficient and it makes sense.

You might think that this new "Partnering" Utopian of a society will drive Men and Women further apart. But eventually the groups will come back together, because we all need each other spiritually.

It won't be long before all of the haters come out of the walls rearing their ugly heads to get revenge for something they felt they deserved but never got in life, lashing out at the content in this book.

> **"All you need is a CoHabi~Couples Agreement. You know, a partnership, partner-riage agreement."**

I wish I could change it for you but I can't. I'm sorry. This is reality.

Now lets get to work at making changes, picking up the pieces and moving towards a "Partner~riage" driven society.

Some partner-riages may last a lifetime. Some may last only weeks. I mean that is already happening, except we have these despicable contracts of marriage and divorce that fuck everything up, for everyone.

If you must approach your relationship with that moniker called "Marriage", then if you live together in a state that recognizes common law marriages, and you don't wish to be married, it's a good idea for you both to agree to (sign) a living together agreement (sometimes referred to as a "cohabitation agreement"), a CoHabi~Couple, Domestic Partnership, or Partner~riage agreement, making it clear that you both intend not to be married and describing your plans for keeping property separate and/or joint and for waiving any right to ongoing financial support from one to the other if you do break up. If you

> **Humans that enter into relationships, need to start putting agreements into place beforehand.**

have kids, you both need to support them 50/50. If income is a concern, then support the kids proportionately.

If you use the same last name and/or mix property together, it's essential that you do this. Otherwise a court might later find that a common law marriage existed, which can affect property rights and in some states, the right to support.

If you have a legitimate common law marriage, and you move to a state that doesn't permit them, your marriage should still be valid. This is because the "full faith and credit" clause of the U. S. Constitution requires states to recognize marriages that were legal in the state where the marriage took place.

As to the subject of same-sex common law marriage, in light of the U. S. Supreme Court's decision legalizing same-sex marriage, in theory these couples should be accorded the right to enter into a common law marriage in those states that still recognize them.

One unique solution that bubbled to the top during this research is that of a CoHabi-Community. Two ladies living together, close to two men living together. The men would connect with the ladies for reproduction, you know "breeders". Both households lived close to each other so that raising the kids became a community effort.

If anything, humans that enter into intimate relationships need to start putting agreements into place before they boink or shack~up.

Marriage Doesn't Work

What Men Need

"...!?... "

~Dick Richard, Random Ghost Author

Men only need three things.

      Sex.

      Food.

      To be left alone.

Marriage Doesn't Work

What Women Need

"One day we will learn how to live without Men."
~Betsy Cocker, Random Ghost Author

Women only need three things.

- Bomb Sex.

- Attention.

- No Bullshit.

- Laughter.

- Friendship.

- Honesty.

- Loyalty.

- Taken care of.

- Protection.

- Puppies.

- Control.

- Recipes.

- Flowers.

- Range Rover.

- Full gas tank.

- Vacations.

Marriage Doesn't Work

Lots of Diamonds.

Real Estate.

Family.

Gooey, Smooshy Love.

Presents.

Children.

Maids.

A cook.

Mani Pedis.

Massages.

Whole foods delivery every 2 days.

Salon visits monthly.

Peloton/Workout Room.

- A massive closet.

- A separate closet for workout gear.

- Always right.

- Win every argument.

- Fuck it... Everything.

Marriage Doesn't Work

Divorce Court Jeopardy

Marriage for $1MM

"Behind every woman is a man not doing what he is supposed to..."

~Bambi von BierSchlampe, Random Ghost

ANSWER: In Western culture, this traditionally follows the honeymoon.

QUESTION: What is a restraining order?

ANSWER: This mammal can consume as much as 300 pounds of food a day.

QUESTION: Who is my mother-in-law?

ANSWER: This is the most common weapon used in abusive marriages.

QUESTION: What are children?

ANSWER: This social movement culminated in the legalization of same-sex marriage.

QUESTION: What is misery equality?

ANSWER: This is the most common complaint wives have about husbands.

QUESTION: What is "Blah, blah, blah. Whatever?"

ANSWER: Male polygamists say this is the worst part of having multiple wives.

QUESTION: What is having multiple mothers-in-law?

ANSWER: This is the leading cause of erectile dysfunction.

QUESTION: What is marriage?

ANSWER: This is the #1 thing wives say they want from their husbands.

QUESTION: What is "I so don't give a fuck!?"

ANSWER: In the worst marriages, this adorns the white picket fence.

QUESTION: What is yellow crime-scene tape?

Divorce for 2x $Marriage

"A man isn't completely finished after Marriage, until Divorce, then he is completely finished..."

~Karina KumpelKasse, Random Ghost

LIFETIME MULTIPLIER

ANSWER: This controversial tactic can be employed to avoid paying alimony.

QUESTION: What is homicide?

ANSWER: Divorced men say this was their greatest regret about their marriage.

QUESTION: What is not cheating more?

ANSWER: This man originated the old saying "happy wife, happy life."

QUESTION: Who is some naive asshole?

ANSWER: This procedure has proven to be less excruciating than marriage counseling.

QUESTION: What is self-immolation?

ANSWER: This is the secret to a happy marriage.

QUESTION: What is a lobotomy?

ANSWER: This is the leading cause of marital strife.

QUESTION: What is stupid fucking women?

ANSWER: These ancient people invented marriage.

QUESTION: Who are morons?

ANSWER: This is the first action a wife should take after filing for divorce.

QUESTION: What is drop dead?

ANSWER: This is the secret to preventing divorce.

QUESTION: What is avoiding marriage?

ANSWER: Amid a contentious divorce, this is the best course of action for the wife's mother.

QUESTION: What is suck cocks in Hell?

Marriage Doesn't Work

Misogyny for $500

"All men make mistakes...Divorced men have learned how to fix them...

~Herr BonkinFunk, Random Ghost

ANSWER: This is the best way to hold on to a woman.
QUESTION: What is by the ears?

ANSWER: This is more painful to men than childbirth is to women.
QUESTION: What is watching "The View?"

ANSWER: This is the #1 barrier to communication between husbands and wives.
QUESTION: What is "Shut your pie hole, bitch!?"

ANSWER: Wives say this is their most important need in life.

QUESTION: What is something to complain about?

ANSWER: This is the #1 sign your wife is a birdbrain.

QUESTION: What is she quotes Oprah?

ANSWER: This is the most important action a wife can take to feel good about herself.

QUESTION: What is shut up and get me a beer?

ANSWER: This is the most important action a lesbian wife can take to feel good about herself.

QUESTION: What is shut up and get me a beer?

ANSWER: This is the most important action a gay man spouse can take to feel good about herself.

QUESTION: What is shut up and get me a beer?

ANSWER: This is the worst punishment an adulterous husband can receive.

QUESTION: What is having it aired on "Dr. Phil?"

ANSWER: This is known as "the estranged husband's best friend."

QUESTION: What is revenge porn and Sex Robots?

ANSWER: Men say this is the most painful result of a failed marriage.

QUESTION: What is dashed dreams of a threesome with her sister?

ANSWER: The way to a man's heart is through this.

QUESTION: What is his zipper?

ANSWER: The two things men think about, and only these two things.

QUESTION: What is Sex and Food?

ANSWER: My Green Martian Penis.

QUESTION: Men are from Mars; women are from Venus, so prepare Uranus for ...

Marriage Doesn't Work

Registered Man Haters for $1000

"All women make mistakes...Divorced men have learned how to fix them...

~Fräulein Saftsaugen, Random Ghost

ANSWER: Even the most unreliable men can be counted on to do this.
QUESTION: What is scratch their balls?

ANSWER: This is the best way to keep a man.
QUESTION: What is under surveillance?

ANSWER: This is the #1 reason men cheat.
QUESTION: What is they're men?

ANSWER: Men commonly confuse big balls with this.
QUESTION: What is small brains?

ANSWER: This is the #1 reason men aren't honest about what they want.

QUESTION: What is because they're liars?

ANSWER: It is easier for a camel to go through the eye of a needle than for a man to do this.

QUESTION: What is put down the toilet seat?

ANSWER: This is the average age at which a man reaches maturity.

QUESTION: What is never?

ANSWER: This is wives' biggest unfulfilled fantasy.

QUESTION: What is husbands washing, folding and putting away laundry?

ANSWER: This is the #1 cause of head injuries in men.

QUESTION: What is they don't listen?

ANSWER: This is why men think they're always right.

QUESTION: What is because they're always wrong?

ANSWER: This is the saddest part of a gay mans breakup.

QUESTION: What is leaving your buddies behind?

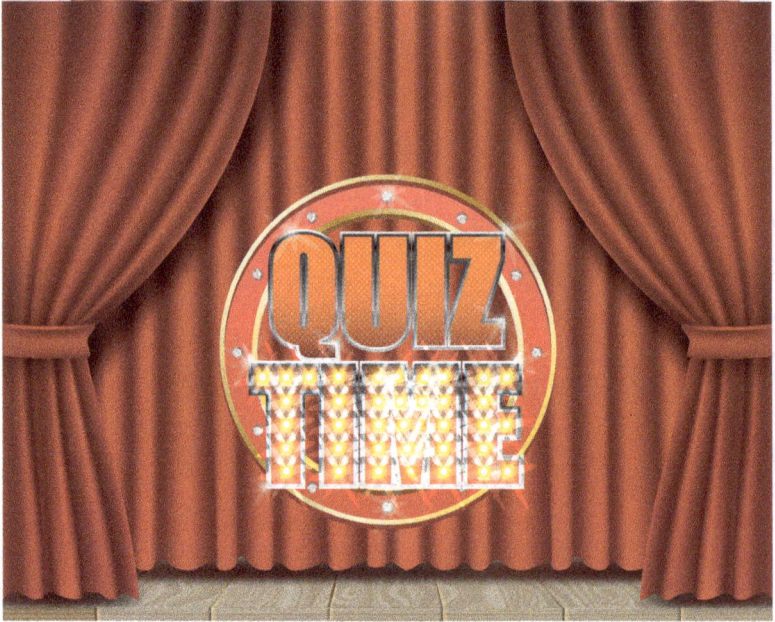

Marriage Doesn't Work

Multiple Choice

Yes, there's a Quiz

"Behind every woman is a man, STILL not doing what he is supposed to...why don't you fucking listen..."

~Bambi von BierSchlampe, Random Ghost

DIRECTIONS: Multiple Choice,
Multiple Answer

QUESTION: Marriage should be renamed to?

ANSWER:

- ☐ The finish line
- ☐ The validate me ceremony
- ☐ Think of all your dreams... now flush them.
- ☐ Let me just buy you a bunch of fucking diamonds and give you all of my shit
- ☐ I'll take the diamonds, a Range Rover, the Real Estate ~ and I don't want your shit
- ☐ Just take everything I have

QUESTION: Divorced should be renamed to?

ANSWER:

- ☐ What is mine is now yours
- ☐ Lawyers and Judges making up crazy shit
- ☐ All Weapons Allowed
- ☐ Let me just buy you a bunch of fucking diamonds and give you all of my shit
- ☐ The Lawyer takes the diamonds, Range Rover, and Real Estate ~ and they don't care about your shit
- ☐ Just take everything I have

QUESTION: The elephant in the room is?

ANSWER:

- ☐ Marriage doesn't work
- ☐ Neither does Divorce
- ☐ Lawyers and Judges making up crazy shit and passing it off as truth
- ☐ Your Ex making up crazy shit and passing it off as truth
- ☐ Falsified DHS reports
- ☐ Falsified police reports
- ☐ Haven't got a clue
- ☐ Elephant, what Elephant?
- ☐ All the above

QUESTION: Fuck it?

ANSWER:

- ☐ Back an '18 wheeler up to TJ MAXX Homegoods and load the whole fuckin store then send me the bill ~ because that still sounds better than what the Judge just fucked me with
- ☐ Pick a different store
- ☐ Pick her favorite store
- ☐ Pick two more of her favorite stores, you're still fucked

QUESTION: Shut the fuck up?

ANSWER:

- ☐ My wife says to me all the time
- ☐ My wife just gives me a look and I #STFU
- ☐ Ok
- ☐ No. Seriously, Shut the Fuck Up
- ☐ Wait, aren't you the bitch likes blueberries?

QUESTION: How did this happen?

ANSWER:

- ☐ Fuck if I know
- ☐ Never seen one of those
- ☐ Never seen two, let alone one
- ☐ Fuck if I know
- ☐ Wait, aren't you the bitch likes blueberries?

QUESTION: Hey Judge?

ANSWER:

- ☐ Fuck you
- ☐ Fuck you again
- ☐ Double, Triple, Quadruple Fuck you
- ☐ And finally, one last time, Fuck You!

QUESTION: Hey Opposing Counsel?

ANSWER:

- ☐ Fuck you, you are a Fucking Liar
- ☐ Fuck you for lying in a court of law
- ☐ You should be disbarred
- ☐ So should the Man Hating Judge
- ☐ I bid you a Final Fuck You, your stolen diamonds, stolen Range Rover, stolen real estate and stolen everything he ever worked for in his life, asshole(s)

QUESTION: You should have signed your Marriage Certificate with?

ANSWER:

- ☐ A Pencil
- ☐ Invisible Ink
- ☐ Disappearing Ink
- ☐ Blood
- ☐ Mud
- ☐ Someone else's signature
- ☐ Ass end of a burning cigarette
- ☐ Ass end of a burning cigar
- ☐ Ass end of a burning tampon
- ☐ WAX seal that says "VOID when the shit hits the fan"

QUESTION: You are buying a wedding present?

ANSWER: It is...

- ☐ A Gift Card for a years worth of therapy
- ☐ A Retainer for a divorce lawyer
- ☐ A Gun
- ☐ Liability insurance for the gun
- ☐ A Shovel
- ☐ Gift certificate to a crematorium

QUESTION: By getting married, you have?

ANSWER:

- ☐ Quadrupled the amount of problems you have to fix
- ☐ Made the worst "legally binding contract" decision of your life
- ☐ Started to try to change another person to the way you thought there were supposed to be before you married them
- ☐ ~~Made the best decision of your life~~ (*Answer no longer available*)

QUESTION: You are buying a Divorce present?

ANSWER: It is...

- ☐ For me, all of it, I'm buying whatever the fuck I want from now on
- ☐ All expenses paid trip to Vegas with your buds
- ☐ A gun
- ☐ A shovel
- ☐ A pitchfork?
- ☐ A cigar - an exploding cigar

QUESTION: Alimony should be renamed to?

ANSWER:

- ☐ Fuck you, get a job, part I
- ☐ Screwing you over is my job
- ☐ I deserve free handouts for the rest of my life
- ☐ Fuck you bitch, you don't deserve this
- ☐ Fuck you dick, I deserve this
- ☐ Legally binding monthly recurring revenue for prostitutes

QUESTION: Child Support should be renamed to?

ANSWER:

- ☐ Fuck you, get a job, part II
- ☐ Kid Rent
- ☐ Bullshit
- ☐ "I should have pulled out" payment
- ☐ Sperm Repository Usury Tax
- ☐ Fuck you, get a job, part III"

QUESTION: Bitch sleeping with your man?

ANSWER:

- ☐ Twatwaffle
- ☐ Bumtrinket
- ☐ Sperm Sucker
- ☐ Coke Whore
- ☐ Beer Slut
- ☐ Skank Ho
- ☐ Homewrecker
- ☐ Child Orphaner

" Something inside of me just clicked, and I realized I didn't have to put up with anyones bullshit ever again "

~ Random Ghost

Marriage Doesn't Work

Random Therapy

Comedy and Satire

"If we can't laugh at ourselves, then we will have to laugh at everyone else..."

~Duke von EselKanon, Random Ghost Author

Neither Does Divorce   411

Marriage Doesn't Work

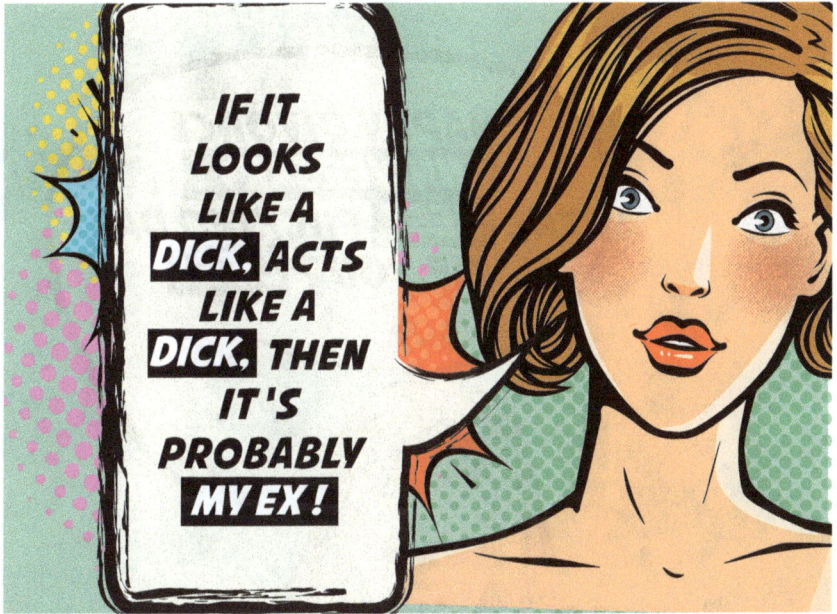

Marriage Doesn't Work

Marriage Doesn't Work

REMEMBER THAT DRUNK GUY LAST NIGHT?
HE LOOKED LIKE HE WAS HAVING A GREAT TIME, WHO WAS THAT?
MY EX-HUSBAND FROM TEN YEARS AGO...
HAHA, SO HE IS STILL CELEBRATING !?

Marriage Doesn't Work

Marriage Doesn't Work

THE WAY PEOPLE TREAT YOU IS A STATEMENT ABOUT THEM AS A HUMAN BEING. THERE IS NOTHING WRONG WITH YOU !

Marriage Doesn't Work

Marriage Doesn't Work

Marriage Doesn't Work

◆◆

Our Sincere Thanks and Gratitude to the Ghost Writers:

Molly Von SchwætzenKüchen (Molly Pussychutte)
Baldrik KräppeSchwänze (Bald Poopy Penis)
Wanda MehrSchittekätter (Wanda more pecker)
Fräulein Müschiküchen (Young pussy cake)
Bambi von BierSchlämpe (Young beer slut)
Duchess von DonnerZünge (Lady thunder tongue)
Karina KümpelKässe (Countin dudes cash)
Firey FickenStar (Hot pornstar)
Fräulein Saftsaügen (Lady sperm suckle)
Hilde Kondom nach dem Drücken (Hilde likes condom after squeeze)
Dr. FüchsViel (Dr fucks alot)
Herr BonkinFünk (Mr weird fucker)
Mama gibt keinen Scheiß (Mommy doesn't give a fuck)
Klutz CuntzschKnaller (Kltuzy cunt banger)
Herr Jünge WankenViel (Young spanker boy)
Rohrmüll PrügelSchlägt (Pipe beater)
Rory SchwänzLecken (Rory dick licker)
Ricard SchläffSchaft (Richard limp dick)
Wilhelm von SüpsenMänn (Dick poke-a-man)
Duke Fick Dichan (Dude, the fuck you lookin at)
Ricard SchwänzBaumelt (Toolboy schlong dangle)
Lord FünkenBütter (idk 🎮)
Billy Arschtherapeut (Lame ass therapist)
Sister Greta NeedHams (Greta need more dick)
Lady Snapdragon (Miss Vagina trap)
Duke von EselKanön (King of the Ass Canon)

#CULT star RISING

CULT STATUS CERTIFIED BEST SELLER

#EXPOSEthe ELEPHANT

#HIDDENgem

ISBN 978-0-9822570-7-4

90000

9 780982 257074

MARRIAGE DOESN'T WORK

· NEITHER DOES DIVORCE ·

Marriage Doesn't Work

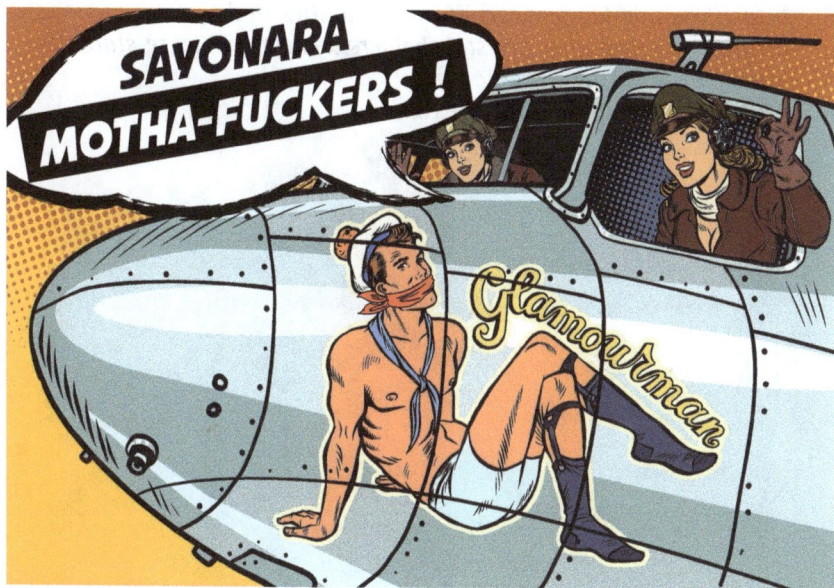

ENDNOTES:

1   Comedian ~ Ghost Writer
2   https://youtu.be/3WMuzhQXJoY
3   https://www.wf-lawyers.com/divorce-statistics-and-facts/
4   https://www.thehotline.org/stakeholders/domestic-violence-statistics/
5   https://www.census.gov/data.html
6   https://www.familylawsoftware.com/

www.ingramcontent.com/pod-product-compliance
Lightning Source LLC
Chambersburg PA
CBHW050231270326
41914CB00033BA/1864/J